MY TWO CENTS

UNSOLICITED WRITINGS ON RACE, POLITICS, & CULTURE

By Agyei Tyehimba

MY TWO CENTS: UNSOLICITED WRITINGS ON RACE, POLITICS, & CULTURE

Dedication

To the "Souljahs of the People," past and present, who speak truth to power, live among the people, and work with the people to achieve and obtain Black Consciousness, Black Solidarity, and Black Liberation....

To the ancestors, the living, and those yet to be born.

To those who diligently follow and read my blog, "My True Sense." Thanks for your support, comments, and for reading my work. Thanks to you, people read my blog in over 150 countries around the world! I sincerely appreciate your appreciation.

To the school dropouts, brothers and sisters in prison, those disconnected from their fathers, gang members, the miseducated, self-hating, abused, neglected and unemployed...The revolution will be **realized**..."*The first shall become last, and the last shall become first.*"

To brothers and sisters killed by racist and inhumane police and white vigilantes.

To George and Adrienne Stith, Harold Stith, Dr. Randolph Hawkins, Dr. Janis Mayes, the Student African American Society and the African American Studies Department at Syracuse University. Dr. James Turner and the Africana Research & Studies Center at Cornell University, Nubia and Zakiya Tyehimba, Illona Wright, Cheryl Wills, Brenda Hillaire, Marc Gates, and other family members, mentors and friends who have given me love, support, and friendship.

To fellow members of the **Black Power Cypher**, four Black men whose intelligence and commitment to family and the Black Nation inspire me deeply: Ishmael Bey, Jerome Walker, Kitwana Tyhimba, and Yusef Bunchy Shakur. To staff and attendees of Harlem Liberation School...

Introduction

In 2007, I and fellow Harlemite Azie Faison wrote a book (*Game Over: The Rise and Transformation of a Harlem Hustler*) about Azie's life as a legendary former drug kingpin. On the surface, this book described the sexual escapades, shopping sprees, and sensational nature of those involved in that lifestyle.

The real objective was larger in scope and far more important. Using Azie's personal story as a backdrop, *Game Over* exposed the role that inner-city drug trafficking played in the mass criminalization/ incarceration of Black people, the mass genocide of Black people, and the socially engineered sabotage of Black political empowerment and Black resistance.

I followed that with *The Blueprint: A BSU Handbook*, in 2013. Drawing from my experience as a college student leader, this book reminded college Black Student Unions of the sociopolitical factors in the United States, which led to the creation of the first BSU in 1966. The book's major objective was to remind BSU why they existed in the first place, and to provide ideological foundations, leadership training, and organizational skills that would help them once again become the radical voice of activism and scholarship on American college campuses.

The following year I wrote *Truth for our Youth: A Self-Empowerment Book for Teens.* The objective of this book was to provide our youth with the character development and emotional intelligence to successfully navigate life and become empowered and empowering adults.

My fourth and latest offering, *My Two Cents*, takes a different approach to my lifelong mission of education, empowerment, and scholar-activism. The writings here are reprinted from my blog (mytruesense.org). My blog's tagline is, *"Raising Consciousness, Challenging Oppression, Inspiring Action."* With 239 entries, my blog has attracted over 100,000 views, close to 2,500 followers and loyal readers from over 150 countries throughout Africa, Asia, Europe, Australia, North, Central and South America, Iceland, New Zealand, the Caribbean Islands, and the Pacific Islands. Most recently, a Black-owned Internet Search Engine named "Huria Search," voted "My True Sense" one of the Best Black blogs on the Internet.

The essays I selected for this book represent the most read, most commented on, or (in my opinion) the most relevant of those on my blog.

Each essay falls into one of three categories in the phrase, "Wake up, Clean up, or Stand up" first articulated by the incomparable Malcolm X. Essays in the "Wake up" section, involve raising consciousness, and providing important analysis of things relevant to Black folk.

The "Clean up" section of the book features writings that focus on critique or addressing our own self-defeating views, values, and practices.

Lastly, those essays that comprise the "Stand up" section of the book contain information and perspectives designed to help Black people solve our problems, and become agents of our own liberation and empowerment.

Those of you who have never followed my blog can see what all the fuss is about. Whether you agree or disagree with my perspective, you will hopefully be inspired and informed.

Those of you who regularly follow my blog, will have a collection of my most important writings in one book. Enjoy these words, implement these words, and please help me to spread these words....

Table of Contents

Part III - Stand Up!

Part I

"Wake Up!"

Raising Consciousness: Becoming aware of who we are, who are enemies are, why/how we are oppressed, and our responsibility to confront our problems and solve them

Black Nationalism 101

Note: It would take an entire book at minimum to adequately discuss and explain Black Nationalism. In fact, several books on this topic exist (I provide a list of some at the end of this essay). If you are looking for a detailed and exhaustive discussion of the topic, this essay is not for you. If you are thoroughly knowledgeable about Black Nationalism, this essay will prove much too elementary for you. This essay, as indicated in the title, is a preliminary and basic discussion of Black Nationalism, for those readers who know nothing about the topic or very little.

Throughout my years as an undergraduate and graduate student, along with my involvement in activist circles, Facebook discussions, and street corner "debates", I have encountered various Black people who harbour negative views of Black Nationalism.

Feminists who are familiar with the misogynist behaviour of *some* nationalists, refer to specific nationalist personalities of the Black Power Movement, and tend to classify nationalism as chock full of machismo, sexist and patriarchal. All-too-often, the dominant image of the ideology is one in which women walk 10 paces behind their male partners, and spend significant time in domestic activities, raising children and silently "supporting their man" uncritically.

In addition, some feminists argue that nationalists obscure women from leadership positions and scarcely attempt any rigorous gender analysis, if any at all.

Members of the LGBTQ community, incensed by offensive references to their sexuality made by "heteronormative" nationalists, characterize the ideology as patently homophobic.

Black people of the Marxist or Socialist persuasion often argue that nationalists focus too narrowly on racial issues and fail to analyze capital and class.

And the cultural pluralists/multiculturalists (along with their leftist counterparts) believe nationalists - with their blanket hatred/rejection of whites - are chocolate-covered racists trapped in a 1960s time warp who subscribe to simplistic and outdated notions of biological determinism. I can hear them now saying in unison, "ALL white people are NOT the enemy." (Incidentally, I find this statement true but very annoying).

In summary, we Black Nationalists are typically mischaracterized as hate-mongers, demagogues, advocates of random violence, misogynists, Black supremacists, and irrational idealists who romanticize an era long gone. It does not help that rigid fundamentalist nationalists behave in ways or espouse views that empower and seem to justify these flawed archetypes.

Because sensational images of nationalists are those most depicted by the corporate media, and since some nationalists themselves give the ideology a questionable reputation, we will attempt to briefly describe Black Nationalism and its different ideological branches. There is not enough space or time here to present a complete paper on Black Nationalism. But I do hope to present the ideology as more nuanced and sophisticated than its critics do, and to challenge the way people sometimes paint the ideology with such broad strokes.

It is important to note that Black Nationalism is not the "evil twin" of pluralism, nonviolence or integration. Nor is it a "Johnny-come-lately" school of thought that first emerged with the rise of Black Power in the sixties.

Actually, Black Nationalism is as old as America itself - older in fact. As James Cone notes:

The roots of Black Nationalism go back to the seventeenth-century slave conspiracies, when Africans, longing for their homeland, banded together in a common struggle against slavery.

It was also found in the rise of mutual-aid societies, in the birth and growth of black-led churches and conventions, and in black-led emigration schemes. Unity as a people, pride in African heritage, the creation of autonomous institutions, and the search for a territory to build a black nation were the central ingredients that shaped the early development of the nationalist consciousness.[1]

And while there are some advocates of nationalism that DO EMBODY MANY OF ITS NEGATIVE CRITIQUES, we should also note that many clear-thinking, balanced and serious-minded individuals championed Black Nationalism from the 19th century until the present: Martin Delaney, Robert Alexander Young, Henry Highland Garnett, David Walker, Henry McNeal Turner, Alexander Crummell, The Honorable Elijah Muhammad, Prophet Noble Drew Ali, Marcus Garvey, Queen Mother Moore, Malcolm X, Assata Shakur, Robert F. Williams, Mutulu Shakur, Kwame Ture, (aka Stokely Carmichael), Imari Obadele, Sister Souljah, and many more.

There is a tendency to view Nationalism in simplistic terms. Yet it has different branches, some conservative some fundamentalist, and others more progressive.

Groups like The Moorish Science Temple or Nation of Islam embody religious manifestations of Nationalism. Such organizations focus on Black solidarity, industry, and a renunciation of chauvinist white religious principles. For example, in such organizations, the Supreme Being is Black and Black people are considered God's "Chosen people."

---

[1] James H. Cone, *Martin & Malcolm in America: A Dream or a Nightmare?* (Maryknoll, NY:Orbis Books 1991, 9,

Organizations like the Black Liberation Army or Revolutionary Action Movement represent revolutionary manifestations of nationalism that advocate armed insurrection and an overthrow of repressive white government. The Black Panther Party, African Blood Brotherhood or the League of Revolutionary Black Workers embody nationalist organizations with a strong critique of class and capitalism in additional to interracial cooperation.

Nationalism often promotes issues of Pan African solidarity, race pride and Black industry as in the case of the Universal Negro Improvement Association. The "US" organization is an expression of cultural nationalism, which emphasizes Blacks' identification with African views and values along with the rejection of European-imposed definitions and standards.

Groups like the Republic of New Afrika as did the Nation of Islam, argued for separatism and sought American territories for Black occupation and nation development. Clearly, the philosophy of Black Nationalism is by no means monolithic.

Nevertheless, we can identify some core concepts of Black Nationalism. Among these are:

- **Self-Determination:** The right for Black people to define their own leadership, values and methodologies.

- **Black solidarity:** Unity around race pride, the common experience of oppression, and common values.

- **Self-reliance:** The formation of Independent Black organizations and institutions that operate in Black interests, and the idea that Black people unify and organize to solve their own problems rather than looking for whites to do so.

- **Race pride:** A conscious attempt to instill pride of African/Black history, culture, perspectives, values and phenotype.

- **Self-Defense:** The right of Black people to defend their lives and property from physical attack (i.e. mob violence, lynching, church burnings, sexual assault). Sometimes, as evidenced by revolutionary nationalists, *proactive* violence against oppressive government agencies is also upheld.

Therefore, some individuals and organizations believe and implement all of the above principles or any combination of the above. As noted, some are more conservative, while others embody ideas that are more progressive. Given the breadth of this ideology, it is inaccurate to assume a person's complete political menu just because he/she is nationalist. Nationalist ideology is interpreted and practiced in vastly different ways.

For example, some Black Nationalists seek separate territory upon which they can create a physical, political and economic nation. Others want a United States of Africa that provides a safe haven for Black people wherever they exist in the world. There are those who believe in developing independent Black political parties and controlling local politics in cities throughout the U.S. Another manifestation of Nationalism includes developing community cooperatives, banks, schools, etc. and operating as a nation within a nation.

In fairness to its critics, Black Nationalism does have its fair share of advocates with half-baked plans, misogynist ideals, oversimplified analysis and cult elements. However, these individuals do not represent the entirety of Black Nationalism. The same holds true for Christianity, Socialism or any ideology.

Perhaps we can learn more about the Black Nationalist tradition, debunk the myths, and develop a more comprehensive and balanced understanding of the ideology. It would surely be tragic if Black people fail to do this, and simplify nationalism as an ideology that teaches that "all white people are evil," or that Black people should use violence indiscriminately. It is erroneous to conclude that nationalism is too narrow and restricted to entertain allies or include an accurate analysis of gender and class. And in a context wherein Black people still find themselves the victims of hate attack, police brutality, poverty, the miseducation of our youth and so many other issues, Black Nationalism remains relevant and useful.

Reading List

- Black Nationalism: A Search for Identity E. U. Essien-Udom

- http://en.m.wikipedia.org/wiki/Black_nationalism

- Classical Black Nationalism: From the American Revolution to Marcus Garvey, Wilson Jeremiah Moses

- Modern Black Nationalism: From Marcus Garvey to Louis Farrakhan, William Van deburg

- Black Nationalism in the United States: From Malcolm X to Barack Obama, James Taylor

-The Ideological Origins of Black Nationalism, Sterling Stuckey

- The Crisis of the Negri Intellectual, Harold Cruise

Understanding the Significance of Malcolm X

In the beginning, the Bible tells us, was the word. But for me, and for the generations that came to consciousness in the 1960's, the Word that created our new beginning (and America's) was "Black," and the not-to-be-trifled-with Giver of the Word was Malcolm X.[2]

Some 46 years after his assassination, Malcolm X remains a much-revered symbol of transformation and uncompromising Black radical leadership. Yet, with his immense popularity comes equally immense confusion and controversy concerning his significance, evolving

[2] William Strickland, *Malcolm X: Make it Plain*, (New York: Viking, 1994),1

political ideology and relevance . . . facts that are underscored because he was killed before he could fully realize his political objectives.

Malcolm's significance arouses hotly contested debate and varied interpretations. Late historian Manning Marable in his controversial biography describes Malcolm X as a combination trickster and hustler figure, who performed several roles in a quest to survive and express himself. According to Marable, "His narrative is a brilliant series of reinventions, 'Malcolm X' being just the best known."

The famed attorney that helped legally dismantle public school segregation and first Black Supreme Court Justice Thurgood Marshall, openly questioned the slain leader's accomplishments: *"I see no reason to say he is a great person, a great Negro. . .What did he ever do? Name me one concrete thing he ever did."* Writer Kevin Pritchett suggested that "Malcolm X did not advocate revolutionary politics but actually the bourgeoisie conservative politics of voter participation, entrepreneurship, and self-accountability." In an inspiring yet disturbing historical moment, one Gallup poll reported that 84 percent of Black people between ages 15-24 regarded Malcolm X as a hero and role model worthy of emulating, *yet few could articulate who he was, and what he stood for.*

---

[3] Vernon Jarret, "Thurgood Marshall Sticks Pin in Malcolm X Balloon," *Chicago Sun-Times*, May 24, 1992, 35.

Kevin Pritchett, "Malcolm X: Conservative Hero," *Wall Street Journal*, November 10, 1992, A24.

[5] http://www.newsweek.com/malcolm-x-196600

Because of the confusion and negative interpretations of Malcolm's legacy and meaning, this essay explores why brother Malcolm stands as one of our most significant and brilliant theoreticians of Black liberation.

Malcolm and the Black Intellectual Tradition

Manning Marable, in his essay "Black Studies and the Racial Mountain," characterizes the black intellectual tradition as being *descriptive, corrective and prescriptive.*[6] Likewise, Malcolm's use of history operated in the same manner. It: 1. Explained the Black experience from the vantage point of Blacks' own perspectives and interests 2. Challenged false and limiting views of Blacks and 3. Encouraged Black people to solve their own collective problems.

It was as if Malcolm X made the Wizard of Oz characters a metaphor for the "brainwashing" confronting Black people in the mid 20th century. Like the scarecrow, some Black people believed themselves to be unintelligent and incompetent. Like the Tin Man, we were "disheartened" and subject to dehumanization. Like the lion, Blacks felt defenseless and emasculated in the wake of white brutality and exploitation. Moreover, we feared taking our rightful places in leadership and positions of authority.

Confronted by these externally imposed views, Black people like Dorothy, were collectively "lost," existing in a geographic and political

---

[6] http://www.columbia.edu/cu/ccbh/souls/vol2no3/vol2num3art2.pdf

landscape both alien to them and hostile to their existence. Malcolm's remedy involved the strategic use of history and re-education to imbue Black people with a reaffirming sense of value and importance, to have Blacks "return home" by embracing their African identity and character, and to deconstruct white supremacy by exposing whites as mere mortals (not wizards) who occupied their position of dominance through coercion and manipulation. His most important weapon toward accomplishing these endeavors would be historical analysis.

Malcolm's "Message to the Grassroots" speech in 1963 is a fine example of his descriptive historical analysis. It is true that his famous comparison of house and field Negroes depicts an oversimplified understanding of captive Africans and plantation dynamics. The house slaves he described as identifying with their masters might have actually been tricksters, feigning loyalty to gain concessions or information. Moreover, as Cornell West suggests, Malcolm's blanket descriptions of house Negroes and their counterparts in the field were not completely accurate or mutually exclusive. Yet his contrast between these enslaved Blacks and their connection to privileged Blacks vs. working class Blacks in the 1960s effectively described Black masses' oppositional relationship to whites, while exposing the placating role often played by Blacks in positions of established leadership.

As Malcolm noted, "Just as the slave master of that day used Tom, the house negro, to keep the field negroes in check, the same slave master has Negroes who are nothing but modern Uncle Toms, 20th Century uncle toms, to keep you and me in check, to keep us under control, keep us passive and peaceful and nonviolent."

Malcolm X was particularly effective and dynamic when using history to correct racist perceptions of Black people. In explaining this he noted,

"When you go back into the past and find out where you once were, then you will know that you weren't always at this level, that you once had attained a higher level, had made great achievements, contributions to society, civilization, science, and so forth. And you know that if you once did it, you can do it again; you automatically get the incentive, the inspiration, and the energy necessary to duplicate what our forefathers formerly did. But by keeping us completely cut off from our past, it is easy for the man who has power over us to make us willing to stay at this level because we will feel that we were always at this level, a low- level."

Accordingly, Malcolm used history in a corrective sense to cite evidence of African civilization and achievement prior to white contact. In his "Afro American History" speech for example, he spoke about Egypt, Mali, Songhai, Ghana, Carthage and Moorish societies as being advanced in mathematics, architecture, and he boldly identified ancient Sumerians and the Dravidian people of India as being Black.

In 1965, Malcolm read the OAAU charter and referred to his new organization's intention to correct the distorted history taught to Black children in American public schools:

When we send our children to school in this country they learn nothing about us other than that we used to be cotton pickers. Every little child going to school thinks his grandfather was a cotton picker.

Why, your grandfather was Nat Turner; your grandfather was Toussaint L'Overture; your grandfather was Hannibal. Your grandfather was some of the greatest Black people who walked on this earth. It was your grandfather's hands who forged civilization and it was your grandmother's hands who rocked the cradle of civilization.[7]

While decades of enlightened scholarship have rendered such commentary commonplace in contemporary times, Malcolm's further call for community-controlled schools, Black teachers and principals, and textbooks written by Black historians comprised educational and historical correctives that were quite progressive and controversial in the 1960s. In addition, we must note that Malcolm, like many of his contemporaries, was influenced by a white slave historiography (shaped by people like Stanley Elkins and Kenneth Stamp) which argued that slavery psychologically and culturally "destroyed" Black people. NOI teachings also promoted this now widely rejected claim. To his credit however, Malcolm did recognize the enormous need for Blacks to use history as a weapon in their fight for identity, revitalization, and empowerment. The **OAAU** charter captures this spirit when it notes: "A race of people is like an individual man; until it uses it own talent, takes pride in its own history, expresses its own culture, affirms its own selfhood, it can never fulfill itself."

Malcolm - in line with his attempt to use history in corrective fashion – often argued that Black people needed to redefine or re-identify themselves. He approached this task in several ways, but

---

[7] http://www.malcolm-x.org/docs/gen_oaau.htm

some of his most brilliant and dynamic efforts in this regard occurred through his rejection of the terms "Negro" "American," and "minority."

Influenced by his **NOI** background, Malcolm X dismissed "Negro" as a derogatory term that expressed contempt and inferiority. Moreover, the term was ambiguous. Speaking in 1965, Malcolm X noted that the term "Negro" lacked any linguistic, geographic, or cultural roots. People that identified themselves as Negroes therefore, effectively disconnected themselves from any history or culture.

Malcolm also chastised Black people for identifying themselves as American citizens. Perhaps the best summary of this idea exists in his 1964 **"Ballot or the Bullet"** speech. Using clever anecdotes, he explains that Blacks do not receive the rights or privileges of American citizenship and reminds his audience that true citizens would not need to protest for the recognition or protection of their civil rights. Lastly, he identifies himself not as an American, but as a victim of America, pointing to an oppositional logic that Black masses should adopt as well: "No I'm not American. I'm one of the 22 million Black people who are the victims of Americanism. . . . And I see America through the eyes of a victim. I don't see any American dream, I see an American nightmare."

The last target of his attack concerning Blacks' re-identification concerned our image of ourselves as "minorities." Malcolm saw this term as particularly disturbing since it caused Black people to view themselves as inferior and incapable of successfully challenging our oppression. According to Malcolm, re-identifying ourselves as a majority would cause Black people to stop privileging whites or viewing them as superiors.

He conceded the obvious point that whites represented a majority population in America, but called for a Diasporic view, noting that African-descended people represented a global majority over whites. He reasoned that American Blacks should align themselves with "the dark masses of Africa, Asia, and Latin America." This, he believed, would inevitably result in the destruction of western imperialism and colonialism in addition to clearing the path to Black liberation in the United States. While his assassination in 1965 prevented him from fully realizing his vision, he was able to do what even Garvey did not, by actually visiting Africa and meeting with various heads of state.

Malcolm X, Black Power and Black Studies

Of all his ideas, Malcolm's call for "a cultural revolution to unbrainwash an entire people" most directly served as a catalyst and reference point for people that would later advocate for Black Studies Programs throughout the nation. Not merely jargon or intellectual abstraction, Malcolm believed education to be a weapon that must be used in the freedom struggle. The Basic Unity Program of the Organization of Afro American Unity reflects his emphasis on education and even anticipates the interdisciplinary nature of Black Studies by noting,

"We must change the thinking of the Afro-American by liberating our minds through the study of philosophies and psychologies, cultures and languages that did not come from our racist oppressors."

Several scholars have already cited Malcolm as the key influence on Black Power ideology and Black student activists, as noted earlier. But is there a direct link between Malcolm X and the Black Studies Movement? On what basis can the call for Black Studies be attributed to Malcolm, ideologically? Scholars like Frederick D. Harper refers to *"Self defense at Cornell, interest in Africa at Princeton, black unity at Northwestern, and black studies and community involvement – all trends of the black students' concerns which depict Malcolm X's charges to black youth and suggest his influence on their behavior."*[8]

Perhaps the greatest evidence of Malcolm's connection to the Black Studies project comes from the stated objectives and personal testimonies of Black Studies advocates themselves. Close scrutiny reveals that their visions for and descriptions of Black Studies closely mirror the ideas articulated by Malcolm X. From his study of 200 Black Studies Programs in 1973, Nick Aaron Ford categorized the objectives of the discipline in the following manner:

---

[8] The Influence of Malcolm X on Black Militancy ,Frederick D. Harper
Journal of Black Studies *Journal of Black Studies* Vol. 1, No. 4 (Jun., 1971), pp. 387-402

- to develop personal identity, pride and worth

- to aid blacks in understanding the basis for an identity that is satisfying and fulfilling

- to develop involvement and improvement in the Black community

- to radically reform American education by attacking its racist assumptions and making it relevant to the current needs of blacks

- to train Black students in the philosophy and strategies of revolution as a prelude to Black liberation

- to promote scholarly aptitude and intellectual inquiry into the Black experience.

Without question, Malcolm X was one of the greatest influences on the Black Power Movement and its prized achievement, Black Studies, Every major player of the Black Power/Black Arts Movements cited Malcolm as a major political/ideological influence.

Maulana Karenga, both a participant in the Black Studies Movement and a prominent Black Studies scholar, outlines five basic objectives of the discipline. These include the intention to teach about the experience of Black people throughout the **Diaspora**, and to "assemble and create a body of knowledge which was contributive to intellectual and political emancipation."James Garrett, who organized the nation's first Black Student Union at San Francisco State University in 1966, and who wrote the first proposal for a Black Studies Department, reiterates the emphasis on Black Studies as a vehicle of Black liberation noted:

"Many of us are coming to understand that we as African people need an educational system which defines objectives in terms of our needs and trains students in the skills necessary to aid in answering those needs. With the rise of national consciousness of African people in America we discover that we must become as independent as possible of the Europeans who colonize us; that we must rely upon our own collective resources as a people to answer our own needs; that we must struggle to destroy the American sphere of influence on the Continent of Africa; and that we must 'render ourselves ungovernable' by those who oppress us."

The students, activists and intellectuals that created Black Studies believed that the educational system developed by whites was hegemonic, and that Black people must develop a system of education that would prepare them for liberation. Nathan Hare, who served as chairperson of America's first Black Studies Department (San Francisco State College) in 1966, wrote several articles explaining the significance of Black Studies. He consistently argued that the discipline should repair the damaged psyche of Black people and equip them with the skills and information to solve problems in their communities. Some white intellectuals viewed Black Studies as being "in danger of becoming revival meetings which may have some therapeutic value but little intellectual substance," or a futile "exercise in racial breast-beating," while advocates like James Turner countered that it would involve serious intellectual inquiry and social correctives that transcended mere psychological revitalization.

When we examine how Black Studies advocates envisioned the discipline, the objectives they articulated for the discipline, and the various issues they debated around creating the discipline, many ideological roads lead back to Malcolm X.

In part, Malcolm's legacy rests upon the legions of Black artists, students, intellectuals and activists inspired by his rhetoric and transformed by his analysis to advocate for self-sufficiency, racial solidarity, and political empowerment and furthermore, to establish independent institutions and organizations to serve these interests. The concept of Black Studies, and the collegiate departments which continue to house and facilitate it, essentially represent an institutionalized pedagogical and intellectual embodiment of Malcolm's call for a critical analysis of the African American and Diasporic experience. The discipline has evolved over time, in some cases developing far beyond what Malcolm could have anticipated, and in other cases, shifting its priorities away from "Black liberation" in its fight to stay relevant and competitive on contemporary college campuses.

Nevertheless, if Black Studies is one of the most important and lasting legacies of the Black Power Movement, then Malcolm X deserves recognition as one of the discipline's important ideological antecedents. By pointing to the development of Black consciousness as foundational to Black liberation, by employing history in descriptive, corrective, and prescriptive fashion, and by arguing for an alternative Black worldview and system of education, Malcolm X in effect, helped to conceive the ideological framework for what would become "Black Studies."He also greatly inspired the many Black Power organizations that emerged after his death including but not limited to, the Republic of New Afrika, Black Panther Party, ₁US, Black Liberation Army and the Revolutionary Action Movement, many of whom literally referred to themselves as the "heirs of Malcolm."

In this sense, Malcolm X indeed "marked" or identified an important reference point on the ever-complex roadmap to Black empowerment, and must be seen not simply as a fiery and uncompromising spokesperson, but a remarkable grassroots organizer and one of the greatest intellectuals and theoreticians of Black liberation in the 20th Century.

Conversation Between the Devil and His Advocates

One day, not long ago, the devil had an executive board meeting with his *devil's advocates* (those agencies/institutions that enforce and implement the wicked plan of deception, exploitation, confusion, injustice and death).

Though generally pleased with their work on his behalf, he wasn't satisfied, and wanted an opportunity to chastise, reprimand and re-motivate his advocates. Hollywood, Education, Law Enforcement, Religion, the Political Establishment, Prison Industrial Complex, Media, Music Industry, and Negro Leadership were all in attendance (The Devil allowed the Financial and Medical Industries to miss the meeting since he believed that those advocates performed their duties *flawlessly*.) The conversation went something like this:

The Devil : "*The Black masses are waking up again, speaking out, learning who they are and resisting MY agenda. This is unacceptable!*

Their knowledge and resistance is costing me MONEY and CONTROL!! I have appointed all of you as my advocates and I expect you to maintain my dominion over the people or ELSE! Have your forgotten your objectives? Each of you reaffirm your allegiance to me by stating your assigned roles....NOW!

Entertainment Industry: "We keep them sedated and distracted so they don't focus on their mistreatment, and persuade them to live vicariously through fictional characters."

Education: "We teach them to obey and defend your authority without resisting it, accept their place as inferior workers in your system, and submit to you for the attainment of power, happiness and prosperity. We also encourage them to disconnect from their history and culture and seek answers and direction from you."

Law Enforcement: "We monitor them, whip their ass, imprison them, intimidate them, and occasionally murder them, to keep them from resisting you."

The Religious establishment: "We keep them wandering in mythology, looking for an external God rather than tapping into the God-force in themselves, and keep them focused on the afterlife rather than life on Earth. We persuade them to do your will while thinking they are doing **THE ALL'S** will. We make them your self-righteous, mindless and contradictory servants.

Political establishment: "We create international conflicts, unjust laws and restrictive rules to keep them fearful, impoverished, powerless, and fragmented. We also give them the illusion that they have input in decision-making, and confuse them into thinking that some of us care about their issues and interests."

Prison Industrial Complex: "We re-enslave them courtesy of the 13th Amendment, exploit their labor like we did that of their ancestors, and make them more effective and powerful community predators."

Media: "We tell the lies you give us in order to help you manipulate people's decisions and behavior through fear and ignorance. We will also determine who/what their enemies are, and teach them to live vicariously through the powerful rather than to become powerful themselves. We will do all in our power to make people with actual solutions and accurate analysis seem foolish and/dangerous. We heighten division and make sure that the habit of independent and critical thinking never gains acceptance or popularity among the masses."

Military: "We teach them to love/serve you, and resent those attempting to organize and liberate them. We use them to help us implement and enforce your global imperialist agenda. We help to destabilize countries and neutralize international leaders or groups that resist your will. We use them to do your dirty work AND kill many of them in the process."

Music industry: "We use the powerful energies of sound and suggestion to fill the people with bitterness, self-directed violence, counterproductive priorities, and criminal desires, all while making money from them doing so. We call this "Operation Pied Piper."

Negro Leadership: "We betray their liberation interests while making them think we are fighting for them. We encourage them to vent without effecting challenging and overcoming your rule. We give them the feeling of making progress and resisting your authority, without actually doing so."

The Devil : "Yes....and don't you EVER forget it! I need more slaves, confused and crushed spirits, mindless robots, bitter and apathetic followers, and submissive workers. I need them to submit to me and reject **THE ALL**...They must NEVER know their power or become Souljahs of the People! Now get back to work, NOW!!

How Racist Propaganda Was Used to Subjugate Black People

Wikipedia defines "propaganda" as "a form of communication that is aimed towards influencing the attitude of a community toward some cause or position by presenting only one side of an argument. Propaganda is usually repeated and dispersed over a wide variety of media in order to create the chosen result in audience attitudes."

It amazes me how much we tend to underestimate the role white supremacist propaganda plays in creating, justifying and maintaining our oppression. Certainly, this phenomenon impacts several groups of people, but my focus in this article is on Black people.

What purposes do white supremacy and racism serve?

All you need do is view Marlon Riggs' pioneering documentary "Ethnic Notions" to appreciate white America's long and systemic effort to thoroughly degrade and denigrate the Black image and psyche. But why so much effort toward this sinister goal? At its core, white supremacy postulates the lie that whites are innately superior to and therefore naturally poised to dominate and oppress Black people. The theory of racism falsely justifies this lie by assigning value and ranking to people based on their presumed racial category.

Naturally, "white" people and those resembling them are assumed superior in almost every form of human expression and activity including but not limited to: beauty, intelligence, ability, leadership, potential, hygiene, health, judgment, ethics, etc.

Racism serves multiple purposes. It provides pseudo empirical evidence to "support" the false claims of innate white superiority and Black inferiority. On one hand, it justifies the negative and discriminatory treatment of original people; it makes the separate and unequal status, opportunities and resources accorded to whites and Blacks seem acceptable and even "natural."

However, people of color are not the sole victims of racism. Racism encourages white people to feel secure in their whiteness although many of them are as destitute, ignorant and powerless as some of their Black counterparts! This false racial consciousness then prohibits such whites from developing a class consciousness that would lead them to organize with people of color around their common labor exploitation and jointly confront their mutual oppressors...the privileged and elite corporate interests which subjugate poor white AND Black people.

Therefore, we see how racism works to divide natural allies, justify brutality and discrimination, and insulate the greedy elite from any real fear of interracial rebellion or revolution.

Why and how is propaganda used against Black people?

Left to their own devices, humans act in their own best interests. No one desires subjugation! Therefore, the only ways whites could exploit our labor, and generally oppress us was to 1) use coercion/force and 2) convince us to become parties of our own victimization through brainwashing and social conditioning.

This second and less coercive tactic took more than a century and ample effort on the part of whites, but had the advantage of being extremely effective once completed. Carter G. Woodson in Miseducation of the Negro, described it this way:

If you can control a man's thinking, you do not have to worry about his action. When you determine what a man shall think you do not have to concern yourself about what he will do. If you make a man feel that he is inferior, you do not have to compel him to accept an inferior status, for he will seek it himself. If you make a man think that he is justly an outcast, you do not have to order him to the back door. He will go without being told; and if there is no back door, his very nature will demand one and cut one to enter.

Forms of racist propaganda used to subjugate us

As explained in the film "Ethnic Notions", or in Donald Bogle's remarkable book, "Toms, Coons, Mulattoes, Mammies and Bucks," anti-Black propaganda manifested into various forms including movies, television shows, toys, board games, nursery rhymes, songs, greeting cards, cartoons, jokes, pictures, theatrical productions, and stereotypes.

Taken together these various mediums portrayed our people as silly, unintelligent, lazy, unattractive, violent, criminal, etc, We cannot underestimate the extent to which these images and characterizations impact how others see us and how we see ourselves today. This is especially significant when you consider that modified versions of these depictions still exist in popular culture today. Spike Lee explored contemporary anti-Black propaganda in his film "Bamboozled."

Common Negative thoughts/practices produced by propaganda

Countless times, I have described this insidious process to friends and co-workers as part of a larger attempt to explain some of our self-defeating attitudes, self-hatred, dysfunction and irritating worship/acceptance of white ideas, symbols and superiority. Not surprisingly, some of us act out the negative scripts written for us by people who despise and seek to control us – and do not even realize we are doing so! Nevertheless, we are conditioned to exhibit many of the following counterproductive beliefs and behaviours:

- Black skin, hair, lips, and body types are ugly or "bad."

- Black people can't organize

- Jewish lawyers are preferable to those who are Black

- The tendency to patronize white businesses over our own

- Our tendency to speak to one another in the most disrespectful ways but act submissive toward whites

- A tendency to disrespect and devalue Black authorities

- A condescending view toward Africa and African people

- Viewing Black institutions or cultural practices as being inferior to their white counterparts

And the list sadly continues. Perhaps no one did a more thorough job of explaining and analyzing the dynamic of anti-Black propaganda than did Brother Malcolm X. Yet several decades after his murder, and the capable contributions of people like Amos Wilson, Naim Akbar and many others, insecurity, identity issues and self-hatred continue to debilitate our organizations, institutions and communities.

What we can do

I am not naive enough to believe that a condition that took over a century to create will end overnight. However, we can do some practical things immediately to counter anti-Black propaganda.

First, we must come to understand how we were/are brainwashed. Second, we can learn the truth about ourselves and our history/contributions.

However, it is not enough for us to simply produce lists of "Black firsts," or "Did you know" Black history. Our history must also be analytical. We do ourselves a great disservice when we cite the past without applying thorough analysis.

Third, we can teach our children to distinguish between propaganda about us and accurate information. Fourth, we should begin to identify, expose and challenge attempts to mischaracterize our people and smear our names. The struggle continues!

Some suggested references:

Films

- Ethnic Notions, Marlon Riggs

- Hidden Colors: The Untold History Of People Of Aboriginal, Moor, and African Descent, Tariq Nasheed

Books

- Brainwashed: Challenging the Myth of Black Inferiority, Tom Burrell

- Breaking the Chains of Psychological Slavery, Naim Akbar

- The Falsification of Afrikan Consciousness: Eurocentric History, Psychiatry and the Politics of White Supremacy, Amos Wilson

- Toms, Coons, Mulattoes, Mammies and Bucks, Donald Bogle

- From Superman to Man, J.A, Rogers

- What They Never Told You in History Class, Induskhamit Kush

- The Miseducation of the Negro, Carter G. Woodson

- African People in World History, John Henrik Clarke

- 365 Days Of Real Black History: Little Known Facts Of The Global Black Experience From Prehistory To The Present , Supreme Understanding

The (Hidden) Agenda Behind Educating Black and Brown Children

Many colleagues, political pundits and administrators grapple with the issue of providing adequate education to this nation's most vulnerable and underserved citizens: children of color. However, while some of us desire to empower and liberate this demographic through education and prepare future generations of leaders and problem-solvers, others have a more nefarious agenda. This agenda disguises itself behind noble-sounding platitudes like "No Child Left Behind," and "Closing the Achievement Gap." Its proponents are conservative and liberal politicians, think tanks, business leaders, educational scholars, and school leaders.

Some have malicious intentions, and others have adopted policies without truly understanding the implications or negative intent.

While Black folk and well-meaning liberal whites comprise much of this last group, some of them also enter the discussion with negative assumptions about Black and Brown students and the larger communities that nurture them. Indeed, some of you reading this have been seduced into supporting (or at least not opposing) this agenda.

Forgive me for pulling the sheet off, bursting your bubble, raining on your parade or refusing to let you drink the Kool-Aid. For you see, *much of the energy and resources behind educational reform in this country are aimed precisely at leaving our children behind* and preparing them to be docile pawns in a game of corporate chess. In this version of the game, Black and Brown people are devalued, regimented, and kept in their place! Is this difficult for you to believe? All you need do is remember the original role carved out for us in this country, all the centuries we have fought against labor exploitation and social injustice, then remind yourself that we all now live in the era of the *New Jim Crow* as legal scholar Michelle Alexander calls it.

The social control of Black people via education is not new. In fact, we can trace its roots to the turn of the 20th Century, when America was a young industrial power, and Black people were only 4 decades removed from chattel slavery. James Anderson in his book, *The Education of Blacks in the South,* chronicles how white liberal reformers, business people and white supremacists alike, participated in a great debate around the question of whether Blacks should receive education and what the scope and objectives of that education should be. These groups held a series of educational conferences to debate these matters. The Capon Springs Conference for Christian Education in the South, convened in 1898 in West Virginia and met two more times in 1899 and 1900.

From these proceedings the Southern Education Board and General Education Board formed. Oil tycoon John D. Rockefeller (who funded Hitler's Nazi Eugenics research movement[9]) founded the latter board, which like its southern counterpart sought to advocate for public education with a *special* role for Black people. You will soon see that while some participants were more malicious than others, ALL of them viewed Blacks as inferior to some degree, and ALL of them saw education as a means to control Black labor and constrain Black political empowerment.

Southern white planters, who held rigidly racist assumptions of Black people, believed that Blacks should not receive any education. They rationalized that education was not necessary for servants and field hands. Additionally they feared Blacks would demand higher wages, political power and generally better treatment if they acquired education. The northern philanthropist and liberal southern whites responded by arguing that education could be used as social conditioning. That is, the *right* education could result in a semi-skilled Black labor force that accepted its place on the bottom societal rung without protest. Carter G. Woodson alludes to this in his classic, the *Miseducation of the Negro*:

---

[9] Schmuhl, Hans Walter (2008). *Kaiser Wilhelm Institute for Anthropology, Human Heredity and Eugenics, 1927-1945* [Dordrecht, Netherlands]: Springer. p. 87

When you control a man's thinking you do not have to worry about his actions. You do not have to tell him not to stand here or go yonder. He will find his 'proper place' and will stay in it. You do not need to send him to the back door. He will go without being told. In fact, if there is no back door, he will cut one for his special benefit. His education makes it necessary.[10]

During the 19th century, Horace Mann, long considered the "Father of American public education" and a strong opponent of African enslavement, advocated a free public education for all citizens. He saw education as an egalitarian means of providing a common and unifying experience for all children. A solid public education would serve to empower and equip citizens regardless of race, religion or origin. However, by the 20th century, corporate barons abandoned his noble vision, choosing instead to use education in hegemonic fashion to maintain and strengthen societal hierarchy.

From 1868-1915, the northern businessmen and southern liberal school reformers therefore became strong advocates of Samuel Armstrong's Hampton University model of education for Black people. Armstrong believed Black people were morally corrupt, unfit for leadership or political power, and in need of "civilization."[11] His curriculum of education for Black people reflected these negative

---

[10] Carter Godwin Woodson, (1990). *The Mis-education of the Negro*. Trenton, N.J: Africa World Press. 21.

[11] *Anderson, James D. (1988). The Education of Blacks in the South, 1860-1935. Chapel Hill: University of North Carolina Press. p. 328.*

assumptions. Hampton emphasized rigorous instruction in social etiquette, hygiene, moral instruction, menial labor and a policy of being complacent and disinterested in political and social empowerment. Armstrong was Booker T. Washington's mentor and Washington adopted his educational policies at Tuskegee Institute. Interestingly, Anderson reports that most graduates of these institutions acquired the equivalent of a 10th grade education and received little actual instruction in skills they could leverage into work.

We can see why W.E.B. DuBois mounted such fierce opposition to these agricultural and technical schools and their agenda of social control for Black people. In his classic book *The Souls of Black Folk,* Dubois asked," Is it possible, and probable, that nine millions of men can make effective progress in economic lines if they are deprived of political rights, made a servile caste, and allowed only the most meager chance for developing their exceptional men?" DuBois argued that the mode of education championed by Armstrong and Washington led to three outcomes:

1. The disfranchisement of the Negro.

2. The legal creation of a distinct status of civil inferiority for the Negro.

3. The steady withdrawal of aid from institutions for the higher training of the Negro. **Footnote**

I argue that the social control agenda of educational reformers exposed by DuBois and Woodson is still in effect today. Moreover, we might view today's educational reformers as the ideological descendants of the 20th century businessmen and liberal (though still racist) whites. In fact, some of the charter school networks we see today were founded by white conservative millionaires. Many of these schools are concentrated does in urban areas with majority Black and Brown people: Albany, Atlanta, Boston, Chicago, Denver, Detroit, Harlem (NY), Indianapolis, Los Angeles, Memphis, Milwaukee, Minneapolis, New Orleans, Newark (NJ), Phoenix, and Washington, D.C.

Sam Walmart – founder of Sam's Club and Walmart's - for example, is a huge financial contributor to the Republican Party. Neither he nor his family have any background of sensitivity to Black or poor people. Walmart's itself is alleged to be predatory, paying its workers significantly below national average, denying benefits, and maintaining a fiercely anti-union position.[12] Yet the Walmart Family Foundation, which supports right-wing causes, has established nearly one in four of the charter schools in the United States, many of them located in Black and Brown communities.[13]

Moreover, let us not forget the teacher-training organization, Teach for America (TFA), which I joined many years ago seeking to become a schoolteacher. This organization took advantage of the great need of school districts to have teachers in the classroom, high rates of retirement for teachers and principals, and

---

[12] https://en.wikipedia.org/wiki/Criticism_of_Walmart

[13] http://prospect.org/article/sorry-walmart-charter-schools-wont-fix-poverty

chronically low-performing schools in urban areas. In the seventies, we called this dynamic "poverty pimping."

TFA recruits mostly young white college graduates, and puts them through an intense and chaotic five-week training program to be teachers. Anyone who has been through this system can tell you its overemphasis on overly punitive disciplinary measures and preparation for state tests.

What many have not thought about is the white paternalism manifested by the subtle "let's civilize the unruly savages" assumptions in such teacher programs. Many will not question why these programs do not adequately prepare their recruits for the challenging educational tasks before them nor how the vast majority of teacher recruits for students of color were not themselves people of color, or people with even a basic understanding of and sensitivity to Black folk and Black issues.

Some Charter schools themselves form a pivotal part of this social conditioning process of people of color. Often created for monetary gain and political influence, many employ inhumane disciplinary practices, rob teachers of union backing and academic freedom, and provide career growth for whites who although (sometimes) well meaning, have little to no educational experience, have racist assumptions about Black and Brown people, and almost no significant understanding of our people. In addition, they provide almost no services for children with special needs and tend to expel them or treat them like threatening inmates.

These schools receive taxpayer's dollars, in addition to private funding and *little outside regulation.* Because they receive public funding, they tend to drain funds that would normally go to traditional public schools, leading to mass public school closings all over the country. Their obsession with test scores and scripted teaching methods robs the joy of learning from our children, whose spirits are crushed as such schools place discipline and statistics over creating future leaders and problem-solvers. Despite the mixed educational outcomes of charter schools, there exists a pervasive myth that charter schools are superior to their traditional public school counterparts. In September of 2015, The Center for Media Democracy put this myth to rest when it published a list of 2,500 charter schools closed for academic and/or financial reasons between 2000-2013.[14]

Whether we examine traditional public schools or charter schools, we must realize that the architects of BOTH (for the most part) DOO do not have positive agendas for Black children. Without radical intervention, the outcomes of such educational models will be exactly what 20th century school reformers wanted: Docile, semi-skilled laborers who stay in their place and remain disconnected from the indigenous communities that produced them. This is the hidden agenda of educating our children. It comes right from the minds and pocketbooks of people who look upon us as people in need of "civilization" and who want to produce effective workers

---

[14] http://www.prwatch.org/news/2015/09/12936/cmd-publishes-full-list-2500-closed-charter-schools

for *their* corporations who will not stand up or speak out against the oppression and devaluation of their people.

What we need then, is a counter educational reform movement. One led by experienced educators, community activists and intellectuals that thinks highly of our students and truly wants to prepare them and their communities to be free-thinking, empowered and community-conscious leaders and problem solvers. The aims of this movement will include:

- A campaign to create authentic k-12 African-Centered schools throughout the country.

- An institution staffed by qualified elder intellectuals and activists that determines accreditation criterion and standards for African-Centered Schools.

- An organization that identifies, recruits, trains, and professionally places effective Black teachers around the country and world.

- A network of education activists, teachers and school leaders that empower parents and communities to better advocate for their children, challenge educationally unsound practices, and make the curriculum more inclusive and reflective of African contribution and perspective.

A Letter From Ime Yamaster to the Negroes of America

{<u>Note</u>: While taking a morning walk months ago in Harlem, I found a diary on a park bench. After sitting there for almost 30 minutes with no one in sight, I picked it up and flipped through it. Inside, I found the name "Ime Ya'master," along with a number of backwards, ignorant, and blatantly racist diary entries. One very long entry, entitled "Letter to the negroes of America," really caught my eye. Insulting but very revealing, the letter I decided, must be shared. Upon returning to my apartment, I tore the pages out, and began the process of transcribing it. This is a reprint of that letter.}

Dear negroes, coloreds, africans, african-americans, nubians, moors, kemites, niggas, etc.:

On behalf of fellow white supremacists, I, Ime Yamaster, write this open letter to address a few points you might find relevant, and to detail some successful initiatives myself and my people believe are best suited for you and your kind.

In light of recent violent "uprisings" among your people, which have led to millions of dollars in property damages, and quite a few injured police officers, I need to inform you of the following. Your inclination to burn businesses, destroy automobiles, loot malls/stores, and initiate acts of violence against good police officers, only underscores your violent, criminal, and confrontational nature. Once again, you make messes all over this fine nation, and white people have to clean it up. Your ungrateful attitudes and actions are intolerable and shameful. If in fact, you find this beautiful country of the United States of America so unacceptable, feel free to self-deport your black asses back to Africa, the Caribbean, South, or Central America!

Certainly, you remember that my ancestors (great explorers, inventors, philosophers, and diplomats) brought you here to assume your rightful place as our servants. Certainly, you also recognize that we, the descendants of those great white pioneers, continue their noble tradition! How any of you can expect us to do you any more favors than we already have, is beyond any reasonable person's comprehension! We freed you from slavery, allowed you to receive some access to college and employment. Hell, we even allowed some of your kind to become elected officials, professional athletes, entertainers, and professionals in all arenas. Some of you are even multimillionaires! What more do you want, considering that we will never allow you to wield power equal to that we rightly hold?

Like spoiled children, many of you bite the superior white hand that provides the lazy and indigent among you with food stamps, cash assistance, medical care, and even discounted housing. We opened the doors of our great universities and allowed some of you to teach, write books, earn good salaries, and **still** you are not satisfied!

You have some nerve to criticize the richest, most powerful nation in the history of the world! Your so-called poverty, broken homes, and academic issues are no fault of ours! Look at notable and accomplished people like Barack Obama, Magic Johnson, Oprah Winfrey, and all the other blacks who have made it in this fine country. If you are poor, hungry, homeless, or ignorant it has nothing to do with me or other upstanding white people. Your laziness and love of complaining and whining rather than working hard and sacrificing are your undoing! Reasonable black people we respect, like Larry Elders and Ben Carson try to communicate this point to you, but to no avail. Stop playing the race card and blaming your social ills on us. If you weren't selling narcotics, shooting up neighborhoods, joining gangs, and making "music" filled with so much profanity and crime, police officers would have no reason to stop and frisk you, arrest you, or restrain you in the first place! Learn how to dress, speak and act, and our police won't have a need to "brutalize" you (By the way, even the more liberal members of my race agree with this, they just won't admit it to your face because they're scared you might attack them).

Since you've proven yourselves lazy, violent, ungrateful, and immature, and since you refuse to accept your place in the social order, my organization helped to create and support several initiatives. I will just list four for now. We've been doing this for years, and most of you still don't have a clue:

1. Negro Disarmament Program: You people are angry and resentful. You probably dream about getting retribution against whites for all the "oppression" you feel we've given you. We intelligent whites know it's just a matter of time before you people begin exercise your second Amendment rights. To prevent you from gaining access to guns, and waging some form of violent revolution or retaliation against us, we've already begun a three-part strategy: 1. Gun buyback programs all over the country in which police precincts pay you money or give you coupons for toys or fast food restaurants in exchange for your guns. We promise you that we will not hold anyone accountable for the guns you bring in, even if some were used for crimes. In truth, we are keeping a record of names and the guns brought in, to use for future raids. 2. Using RICO laws, and "War on Drugs" laws, our police departments launch drug raids against known inner-city drug syndicates in this country. When we have a successful raid, we hold press conferences bragging about all the drugs we confiscated. But we don't give a damn about you selling or using drugs, we really want the money and the automatic weapons you have! We use the money to better arm our police, sell the drugs back to your drug dealers, and distribute the confiscated guns to police, race-loyal vigilante groups, and negro street gangs to aid you in killing each other. 3. In coordination with one of our top race-loyal organizations (the NRA), we pass gun control laws that make it nearly impossible for almost anyone other than white men, white law enforcement officers, white women, and property/business owners to legally apply for and receive a gun permit.

2. Gentrification and colored people's displacement. By making rents more expensive, lowering wages for workers, busting worker unions, and modifying tenants' rights laws, we create mass evictions. Then we lower rents in other sections of the city to force you people into what you might call modern-day reservations and open the door for more of us to live in your neighborhoods, where we begin to control the business, real estate and political structure. Because we turn formerly all-Black neighborhoods into mixed or predominantly white ones, we also make it almost impossible for your people to vote or organize along racial lines. In New York City for example, we've used these methods to force more of you into the Bronx. Check the statistics. Why do you think the Bronx has the highest drop out rates, levels of gang activity, AIDS patients drug addicts, infant mortality, unclean water, rodent problems, and unemployment rates of any borough in New York City? Not an accident!

3. Expansion of our prison initiative. You think the 13th Amendment freed your people? Wrong! Read it again and you will notice that we created a new form of slavery called "incarceration." We will gladly pay $50-$70,000 a year to keep every inmate out of school, deprived of owning a business, unable to vote, and off the streets where you will continue to attack good white people! We also make you work nearly for free, making products that we then sell in the open market! Thanks largely to our "War on Drugs," and "War on Terrorism," we create all types of reasons to arrest, harass and imprison you. Our schools barely teach you enough to think, get a job, run a business or solve problems, so many of you will fall right into this trap. And once you do, we got you! A prison sentence for colored people is really a business contract detailing how many years you'll give us (almost) free labor. For every prison we build and you enter, we create hundreds of jobs. Then we build these prisons in mostly white areas and then count your inmates as part of the population so these white towns can receive more money to educate our children and put our people to work.

4. Operation Pied Piper: It may surprise you to learn that we white folk study you people well. We know you better than you know yourselves! For example, we know how much you love music and comedy and how much these things influence you. Like the childhood story of the Pied Piper, we use music and sound to lead you to your own demise! We started a preliminary experiment in the 1970s. You people were angry and organized during the 60s and mid 70s, and were threatening to upset the balance of power. Our social scientists noted how your music helped to inspire pro-black feelings. Curtis Mayfield, James Brown and other artists created music that taught pride, solidarity and changing our system. We responded by creating a worry-free form of music called "Disco" and peppered it with messages supporting drug usage, apathy, pleasure-seeking, irresponsibility and having fun. This effort, along with our "Poppy field Program" (introducing heroin, "pot" and cocaine to urban areas), and our Counterintelligence Program helped to kill that militant mood and the organizations and individuals that promoted it. When we saw this mood resurface in the 80s, we reinstituted "Operation Pied Piper" on a much larger scale. Our target was Rap music. By the mid-80s, we witnessed black militancy, references to Malcolm X and the Black Panther Party in a variety of music by rap artists. Rappers began talking about black solidarity and black power. On both coasts of the U.S., rappers united to begin stop the violence and gang truce records and concerts. By 1989, we introduced gangster rap on the West coast and hustler rap on the East. IN later years, we also infiltrated rap music in the South. Using your own artists, directed behind the scenes by our label-owners and corporations, we slowly defused political rap music and introduced messages of murder, crime, glorification of prison, disrespect of women, drug selling and drug usage, self-hate, and a rejection of education and political movements. Even now, this remains one of our most successful initiatives, despite attempts from some rappers to perform uplifting material.

As you can see, these plans are working **PERFECTLY**. They destabilize you and empower and enrich **us**. Since we've compromised most of your leadership through bribes, good jobs, and threats, we have every reason to believe you will continue to do our bidding, stay confused and disorganized, and fight yourselves while we manipulate and exploit ALL of you.....

White power and White solidarity always,

Ime YaMaster

A Word About Voting and Politics

Whenever a Presidential election approaches, we all hear the common refrain reserved especially for times like this: "Our people fought and died for the right to vote, and we do our ancestors a disservice if we don't." If one of us brave souls dares to express skepticism about going to the ballot box we hear the equally common *"Well if you don't vote, you don't have the right to complain"* or *"How dare you? Our people bled and died for the right to vote!*

Because I believe such statements are misleading, inaccurate, and potentially counterproductive for Blacks and other oppressed people, I am devoting some time here to address the issue.

My premise is that voting is one of many important citizenship rights we have, and arguably not the one that Black people spent most of their energy fighting for or utilizing. Nor has voting been the most effective and productive tool in our historical arsenal. A proper reading of history will demonstrate that the primary things we "fought and died for" included recognition as United States citizens; having our citizenship rights and privileges enforced and protected; having the artificial barrier of race removed in any evaluation of our ability; being free to fairly prepare or compete for employment, education, business, and other opportunities for "life, liberty and the pursuit of happiness"; and being protected from mob attack, lynching, or various forms of white intimidation and physical brutality.

While many of us today might give particular prestige and privilege to using our right to vote, history demonstrates that Black people have traditionally used many of our other fundamental rights (assembly, free speech, free press, protest) to advance our issues and interests. In fact, we have used this multitude of rights even more than the right to vote in addressing our grievances, a fact we often dismiss in our effort to drum up support for presidential elections.

One natural right Black people have often utilized is that of physically resisting oppression. Though controversial with his theory of "benevolent" slave owners, Eugene Genovese in *Roll Jordan Roll*, documented several accounts of enslaved Africans that broke tools, participated in work strikes, deliberately slowed down their work production, and escaped from captivity.

Herbert Aptheker in his important book *American Negro Slave Revolts* used "government archives, personal letters (sometimes published in distant newspapers), journals, diaries, and court records" to chronicle a 200-year history of Black-led revolts, uprisings, and rebellions on southern slave plantations. In a display of self-reliance, Black people also created their own institutions to address their needs in a nation that neglected them.

According to education scholars Hillary J. Moss and James Anderson, Black people as early as the mid-1800s created their own schools. This occurred during enslavement, during and after the Reconstruction, and often several decades before our right to vote was recognized.

During the 19th century, Black people were formidable opponents of slavery and some emerged to play important roles in the abolitionist movement to end the institution. We can use the Black Abolitionist Archive[15] to search over 800 speeches and 1,000 newspaper editorials by abolitionists such as Frederick Douglass, Sojourner Truth, Henry Highland Garnett, Maria Stewart, Ellen Watkins and many others. Concurrent with abolitionism was the National Negro Convention Movement. Utilizing their right to peaceably assemble, free Blacks held conferences throughout the country where they discussed and debated the problems, needs, and interests of free Blacks and explored methods of improving their condition which included emigration to other countries.

---

[15] http://research.udmercy.edu/find/special_collections/digital/baa/

Utilizing their freedom of the press, Black intellectuals launched Black-owned newspapers like *Freedom's Journal, The Colored American*, and *The North Star*. These mediums became important mediums to disseminate Black news, challenge racist American policies and practices, and energize Black protest throughout the U.S.

During the post-WWI period, Marcus Garvey and his Universal Negro Improvement Association created Black businesses, and the Negro World Newspaper, while calling for Black people to build everything they needed for their own survival and liberation and to free Africa from white colonial control.

During this same period, Black socialist Cyril Briggs created his organization the African Blood Brotherhood and *The Crusader* magazine that called for liberating Africa, increased Black unionizing, and anti-imperialism. Beginning in the 1930s, the Nation of Islam created their own system of schools, vast network of businesses, farms and factories, and through Brother Malcolm, Muhammad *Speaks* newspaper. Dr. W.E.B. DuBois launched and edited *The Crisis* Magazine for several years, which became an equally important medium of political critique and news for Blacks throughout the nation.

Some 40 years later, we witness the Civil Rights Movement's brilliant and courageous use of non-violent protest and grassroots organizing to dismantle formal segregation in schools, businesses, public facilities, etc.

Influenced by the nationalist teachings of Malcolm X and the unrealized promises of the Civil Rights Movement, Black students, intellectuals and activists launched the Black Arts and Black Power Movements, calling for a Black aesthetic, self-reliance, self-determination, and self-defense. Poets like Haki Madhubuti, Sonia Sanchez, Gil Scot Heron, The Last Poets, Nikki Giovanni and Amiri Baraka utilized their freedom of speech and press to speak and write moving critiques of white supremacy and calls for Black solidarity.

Organizations like the Black Panther Party, US, Republic of New Afrika, and Revolutionary Action Movement, drew from socialist, nationalist, and Pan African ideas to create Black schools, medical clinics, community patrols, and a holiday (Kwanzaa). They argued for a separate territory upon which Blacks could live.

This abbreviated survey of our history describes our multi-layered use of protest, rebellion, political writing and speaking, grassroots organizing, and Black-owned institutions/businesses as avenues to empower ourselves. These methods in fact were the dominant and primary methods we used to advocate for ourselves during our long sojourn in America.

This is not to say that we did not fight for the right to vote. However, if we are going to reference our struggle for this right, we should be able to explain *when* and *how* we fought for the franchise. Our right to vote was recognized with the ratification of the 15th Amendment in 1870, but was largely neutralized by white vigilante violence, gerrymandering and the unfair use of grandfather clauses[16] and poll taxes. Consequently Black people did organize to

---

[16] http://www.blackpast.org/aah/grandfather-clause-1898-1915

fight for the right to vote which culminated in The Selma marches of 1965[17] the 1965 Voting Rights Act signed by President Lyndon Johnson and the formation of The Lowndes County Freedom Organization in Alabama which served as a Black political party in 1966. We can conclude that some of our people *did* fight and die to secure voting rights.

This however does not mean that presidential politics has been the salvation of Black people. Our history illustrates in dramatic fashion that Presidents have been reluctant allies to Black progress, if allies at all. In those cases when U.S. Presidents did involve themselves in Black affairs, they did so because of our organizing, critiquing policies, protesting and creating alternative structures (and let us not forget *threatening* them with potential violence and disorder). President Franklin Roosevelt desegregated U.S. defense industries in 1941 only *after* A. Phillip Randolph threatened a massive Black march on Washington in the same year; 30 years of successful litigation by the NAACP forced the Supreme Court's hand, leading to the Brown v. Board desegregation decision of 1954; Black protest in Birmingham, Alabama (1963) exposed southern white brutality around the world, disgracing America's Cold War image as a democratic and inclusive nation. This dynamic pushed John F. Kennedy off the fence, forcing him to deliver the famous address insisting that "A great change is at hand, and our task, our obligation, is

---

[17] https://en.wikipedia.org/wiki/Selma_to_Montgomery_marches

to make that revolution, that change, peaceful and constructive for all." This led to Kennedy's proposal for a Civil Rights Bill;

Scores of Black rebellions in American cities led Lyndon Johnson to sign the 1964 Civil Rights Act desegregating public accommodations, and leading him to form the Kerner Commission[18] in an effort to discover why these rebellions occurred, and develop means to stop them. The recommendations of this commission led to several job-training programs and wide scale Black enrollment in white universities. Ultra-conservative Ronald Reagan signed the bill calling for a National Martin Luther King holiday in 1983 *after* a movement for this holiday led by Stevie Wonder and Coretta Scott King produced 6 million petition signatures. **Our progress has always come from our sustained organizing, protest, and self-reliance.**

In conclusion, I am not advocating that we abstain from voting in national elections. Everyone has the right to utilize or not utilize the right to vote as they see fit. I am suggesting that presidential elections are not the only game in town, are not the most effective means for implementing change, and that we must pursue alternative means to advocate for our empowerment. Given the increasing role of corporate campaign contributions[19] in determining electoral victory,

---

[18] "'Our Nation Is Moving Toward Two Societies, One Black, One White— Separate and Unequal": Excerpts from the Kerner Report." History Matters.**http://historymatters.gmu.edu/d/6545**

[19] https://en.wikipedia.org/wiki/Citizens_United_v._FEC

and in politicians' being beholden to corporate interests, my point is even more valid.

Instead of investing so much of our energy on national elections, we might consider holding the *thousands* of public offices in our local and state governments! These public offices affect our lives in very practical ways (schools, zoning, social services, policing, business contracts, etc.) Yet even this strategy will prove shortsighted and ineffective if we fail to mount sustained grassroots pressure, build economic power, and create institutions that we control.

Unless the present American political party system undergoes radical structural change, I will continue to view voting in national elections as more of a *symbolic* act than a substantial one. I will continue to see it as a fraudulent exercise designed to fool American citizens into thinking that they actually have input in their government.

The growth of corporate influence, military influence and press influence make such elections a joke and a farce. Sure, many Democrats and Republicans disagree on specific issues like abortion, taxes, gun control and the role of government in the lives of citizens. However, on a whole range of other issues, their areas of disagreement are fuzzy. Moreover, this is generally true regardless of a particular candidate's race, gender or class.

If you remember the famous "Peanuts" cartoon, this government is like Lucy holding the football and we are Charlie Brown. We know that Lucy always pulls the ball away when we attempt to kick, but we naively continue to do so. Politics is not moved by appeals to morality but by economic and political power, lobbying and leverage. We must direct our attention to amassing this power, run in local elections, build powerful businesses and institutions, and continue our tradition of protest and resistance.

Racist Police Brutality: History of the American Police State

With the escalation and re-emergence of racist police brutality in the United States, the media, civil rights groups, and concerned Black citizens find themselves discussing and organizing to confront the American terrorist police state. By "police state" I refer to the law enforcement, legal, and political power structure and how they work together to use terror, fear, propaganda, murder and captivity to oppress and control dissent and political organizing among the masses. This agenda reveals itself on American streets, within Congressional legislation, imperialist foreign policy, and within the prison systems of this country.

The Trayvon Martin killing and Eric Garner's murder-by-chokehold, along with the unjustifiable slayings of Michael Brown, Renisha McBride, and Jonathan Ferrell, (all committed by white men in or out of uniform), bring us back to conversations about racist violence against Black people in the United States.

As Hip Hop legend Jay Z has said, "Men lie and women lie, but numbers don't." Nor do numbers lie concerning Black death by white hands. According to the 2012 "Operation Ghetto Storm" report by the Malcolm X Grassroots Movement, statistics taken between January and June of that year demonstrated that a *"Black person was assaulted or killed every 28 hours by white police, security guards or self-appointed vigilantes."*

Disturbing data like this compels the intelligent and concerned among us to ponder why Black lives in so-called "post-racial America are still criminalized and devalued. All across this country, Black people seething with righteous indignation are protesting and discussing how to protect ourselves from agents of the American police state.

Concerning this question of resolution, I have heard and read intelligent and well-meaning Black folk offer the same traditional approaches we always hear regarding police brutality: Marches, demonstrations, rallies, protests, teach-ins, filming police, police sensitivity training, clinics on how to cooperate with and peacefully engage police, and the like. While I am not completely resistant to these strategies, I am admittedly skeptical.

Somehow, we have come to believe that murderous and repressive police act outside of their official duties. And this is where we are wrong. The first intelligent step toward ending or at least effectively neutralizing police brutality is to understand the sociopolitical role and function of police in the United States.

Understanding the true role of police in our nation requires that we know the true history of police forces in this country. Mainstream scholars of police history spin the narrative that America inherited its idea of policing from Britain in the form of constables and night watchmen. According to most accounts, early forms of public policing began first in Boston (1636), then New York City (1651), and then Philadelphia (1705). As populations grew and territories became more industrial and based on specialized labor, other cities adopted volunteer, later professional, and more organized police departments.

This history is factually accurate, but does not explain the political and sociological function of police in modern society. For this, we must dig a little deeper and examine the development of police institutions in the early South. As you will see, this history helps us understand that **police brutality is a mandated, deliberate, and organic part of the U.S. empire.**

The advent of contemporary police departments, if we trace its southern origins, began with slave patrols in the colonies and later states of America. As revealed in the article, *"The History of Policing in the United States: Part I,"*

> *Slave patrols had three primary functions: (1) to chase down, apprehend, and return to their owners, runaway slaves; (2) to*

provide a form of organized terror to deter slave revolts; and, (3) to maintain a form of discipline for slave-workers who were subject to summary justice, outside of the law, if they violated any plantation rules. Following the Civil War, these vigilante-style organizations evolved into modern Southern police departments primarily as a means of controlling freed slaves who were now laborers working in an agricultural caste system, and enforcing "Jim Crow" segregation laws, designed to deny freed slaves equal rights and access to the political system.[20]

Writing in an *article* for *Rebel Press*, Auandaru Nirhani reminds us that:

The US police force was modeled after the British Metropolitan Police structure; however, the **modus operandi** *–especially when policing poor working class, migrant, brown and black neighborhoods– in the present, resembles the procedures of the 18th century Southern slave patrols, which developed from colonial slave codes in slave-holding European settlements in the early 1600s.[21]*

We should add that white vigilantes and their organizations also played a role in "policing" Black people. In 1865 for example, former Confederate soldiers formed The Ku Klux Klan to intimidate and brutalize newly freed slaves and derail the political and social progress

---

[20] http://plsonline.eku.edu/insidelook/history-policing-united-states-part-1

[21] http://therebelpress.com/articles/show?id=2

afforded Black people during the Reconstruction era. Vigilante groups like the Klan, the White League, and the Red Shirts hung Black folk, burned Black churches down and terrorized Black homes in an effort to deter us from voting, organizing politically, and enjoying the rights of U.S. citizens.

In short, white citizens deeply feared the threat of Black power and Black rule so they aimed to solidify white male control of the United States. Often times, these racist vigilante groups worked closely with established law enforcement agencies and more often than not, counted sheriffs, police officers, elected officials, attorneys, and judges as members.

Not just the legal establishment, but political powers-that-be worked in conjunction with police and vigilantes. In the 18th century, the Georgia colony passed legislation requiring that plantation owners and their white male workers join the Georgia Militia. This militia was required to do monthly patrols of slave plantations looking for weapons among slaves and to repel revolts or escape attempts.

While many of us can cite our Second Amendment rights, we do not often think about the motives that led to the amendment. The "white founding fathers" of the United States, especially those from the South, were slave owners who lived in constant fear of Black insurrection. It is no surprise then that these men passed the Second Amendment authorizing the right to bear arms for the maintenance of militias. In school, we were taught that the second Amendment protects citizens from corrupt government forces (a fact we should strongly consider in any discussion of police brutality!) Nevertheless, never forget that a key role of this amendment and its support of armed militias was to monitor and control slaves, and prevent or repress slave revolts in the South.[22]

In conclusion, as far as we are concerned, the broken bones, bruises, spilled blood, paralysis and death we suffer in addition to the tear gas, pepper spray, stomping, chokeholds, bullets and billy clubs unleashed on Black bodies throughout contemporary America are nothing but modern-day manifestations of racist slave patrols.

Acknowledging this fact brings us to the logical conclusions that 1. Black people are to a large degree, perceived and treated by state agents as neo-slaves, people whose labor, mobility, and freedom is subject to control. 2. We are therefore seen as physical and political threats by the established order, which both explains why we continue to be unfairly criminalized and subject to physical attack by law enforcement agents (and even white vigilantes) on any given day. 3. While decent and fair-minded police officers of all racial and ethnic origins do exist, the police department is an institution that "serves and protects" certain class and race interests, and their repeated acts of brutality against us are not incidental or arbitrary, but constitute a mandated, deliberate and organic part of the American social order.

The sooner that we understand this, the better we will be. Our tactics will also improve, as we discard bourgeoisie notions that speaking properly, dressing better, teaching police officers to be

---

[22] Excellent article at truth-out.org entitled "The Second Amendment was Ratified to Preserve Slavery."

"sensitive" or educating ourselves, will in any way deter the American police state from spilling our blood. WE are not the problem. The racist and belligerent American police state that unfairly criminalizes and murders our people is the problem. Up to this point, Black people have experienced great physical and emotional pain with little recourse. Perhaps it is time to explore other options....

Why Whites Defend and Justify Police Brutality

When crisis occurs on a huge level, we can respond in several ways. We can crumble under the pressure and bury our heads in the sand, we can become bitter or self-pitying, or we can analyse the situation, learn from it and more forward with a plan of action.

No one would disagree that the ongoing issue of police officers killing Black people with impunity is a crisis on a HUGE level. Rather than becoming bitter, self-pitying or indifferent, I suggest we see this issue as a teachable moment (in addition to resisting it at every turn).

Every time a police officer murders a Black person in the United States and faces no adequate punishment for his/her deed, we protest or cry out for justice. Whites collectively respond to our protest, usually in resentful and non-sympathetic ways. We can learn much about the nature of this country via white backlash to Black resistance.

This phenomenon reveals much about white supremacy, the perception of Black people, and whites' own political naiveté.

The tragic and unnecessary murders of Trayvon Martin, Eric Garner, Michael Brown, Akai Gurley - and in a separate but related issue - New York City police officers Rafael Ramos and Wenjian Liu, teach us about the issue of police brutality and its related consequences. However, our lessons do not stop there. These tragedies also lift the curtains of white American psyche and reveal disturbing attitudes, perceptions and instincts that forcefully explain the significance of race in our society and why racial injustice will likely be here for some time to come.

First, we must understand that police brutality is not a new or modern phenomenon for Black people. State-sanctioned and organized violence has always been the "enforcer" or "muscle" behind white supremacist policies. This began centuries ago when whites first invaded the African continent to snatch Black people for purposes of enslavement. It manifested again when European powers colonized the continent, and used indigenous labor to mine the soil for diamonds, gold, rubber and other resources to jump-start European industrial growth. Whether under the guise of enslavement, colonialism, imperialism or modern inner-city occupation, military force was/is a constant. The only differences were the uniforms, weapons, language, dialect used or time period employed in question.

Why was military force so crucial? Because no one wants to be exploited, enslaved or mistreated. People will rebel, resist and refuse to cooperate with their subjugation. White supremacists therefore **needed** coercion to control our wealth and labor and intimidate us from mounting any resistance to their efforts. Police - despite what we learned in school - do not actually exist to "protect and serve" the poor or marginalized. They exist to protect and serve state power, policies and property. They exist to monitor, intimidate, and control the masses so that the corporations and government can run smoothly and safely with minimal glitches.

This is not to suggest that modern police do not provide important services to non-affluent or well-connected citizens. They do intervene in domestic disputes and help to prevent or solve a variety of crimes. Society does require some degree of safety and order, as complete chaos is *bad for business*. In addition, an aspiring police state in a "leader of the free world" nation like the United States must carefully camouflage its sinister intentions, lest it lose face throughout the world and lead the masses to initiate full-scale revolution. When we challenge police brutality then, we confront more than police violence; we also challenge the very nature and structure of U.S. empire which we must radically transform. It's tactics and practices need reforming, but even farther, the nation and its police force will need to be rebuilt with vastly different objectives, values, and priorities.

In fairness, we must concede that several thousands of whites in this country acknowledge and oppose the disproportionate assault and murder of Black people by police officers. In city after city, whenever protests occur, we notice ***mixed*** crowds, with whites chanting, marching, "dying-in" and being arrested, alongside Black folk. Regardless of our political ideology, we cannot simply assume people's politics based on their racial identity. We cannot easily place people in rigid categories or sides regarding the issue of police brutality. For example, we know of police watch groups and activities supported largely by white activists, and regular citizens. Their struggle and sacrifice are duly noted and appreciated.

Nevertheless, why do so many whites justify and support the very police forces that mistreat and kill us? Why do so many blame us for being attacked and killed? In addition, what does this tell us about this country and about the nature of white supremacy? These are the questions of the hour, and here are some answers to think about:

- Many whites even when presented with the statistics and other evidence refuse to acknowledge anti-Black police brutality. This denial is sometimes psychological. Such whites do not want to admit that this country still mistreats Black people because they desperately need to believe that this country, and by extension themselves, are as fair-minded, and good-hearted as they proclaim they are. How else can people rail against human rights abuses in other nations and psychologically distance themselves from their own equally inhumane behavior? How else can they salute the flag, and praise American military campaigns against the "bad guys" overseas? In the divisive game of us vs. them, privileged whites need an outsider to oppose. Therefore, whites' insensitivity to us meets a psychological need.

- Some whites don't empathize with the pain and suffering of Black people because deep down inside they believe the racial stereotypes classifying Black people as violent, criminal and prone to exaggeration about racial injustice. In other words, when a cop assaults or kills one of us, they believe that we deserve it.

- The white establishment has long worked to separate whites and Blacks and encouraged even poor whites to have antagonistic relations with Black people. There was a time - the period during which the "United States" was a collection of British colonies - when **poor whites and Blacks fought together** to defeat the rich white planter class in the U.S. Privileged whites responded by legally punishing poor whites that sympathized with Black resistance rather than enjoying and defending their racial privileges. This created a false sense of alliance among poor whites with privileged white elites against Black people with whom they shared class oppression. Creating rigid racial and class divisions among poor whites and Blacks serves the elite's interests, as they can prevent possibly revolutionary interracial class alliances between Blacks and whites, and maintain control over both groups. In this sense, whites have been duped.

- Many whites have a deep-seated fear of Black violence and retribution. Given the opportunity, they believe, Black people will harm or kill them in retaliation for all the years of white discrimination, brutality and exploitation. They see the police then, as their security blanket against Black insurrection and therefore are prone to support and defend them. This also explains the exaggerated media, financial support, and "hero" status awarded to slain officers Ramos and Liu. This becomes necessary to both support American values and reverence for the police.

The verdict is clear. Not everyone shares our perspectives, values and interests. There will be times when whites and our own people are unwilling or unable to "get it." In the case of whites, this is because they derive privilege and status relief from our subjugation. Our people cower in fear of their enemies, in addition to naive and unreciprocated feelings of humanitarianism and "oneness." Nevertheless, our struggle is a righteous one, and we must wage it regardless of outside vindication or dissension from family members OR outsiders. Simply put, white folks do not get to decide what Black people get upset about or how we choose to express our outrage. Black lives DO matter, and no one, cop or otherwise has a license to kill us with impunity.

We are tired of people's attempts to decide which of our issues is 'worthy" of our attention or to champion and defend those responsible for our death. We are tired of being pressured to grieve for others or empathize with their pain, when NO ONE GRIEVES FOR US! When the two NYC police officers were killed, they were labelled "heroes," flags flew at half-mast, and every media personality described their murders as "executions" or "assassinations." The city began raising money to pay off the mortgages of their wives and children. Who cries for us? Who acknowledges our humanity and right to live? It is insulting that when our people are killed we have to defend why they did not deserve to die! Police officers lives are no more precious than the lives of civilians. Nor will we allow whites to determine our political priorities or "heroes."

The sad reality here is that for all the so-called "progress" everyone tells us we've made, white supremacy, along with its insulting assumptions, perceptions, and unwritten truths, is alive and well. It is infuriating to know that the average person will get more jail time for killing a DOG than they will for shooting and killing an unarmed Black man. Just ask Michael Vick. This fact, and the fact that white folks derive privileges from this racist state of affairs, practically guarantees white supremacy's longevity. It is not just a simple matter of life and death, but of privilege, identity, and values. That is the grand lesson here. Black lives, in far too many instances only matter to Black people.....

How the Wizard of Oz Applies to Black People

I am a huge fan of movies and music. In fact, I often think in terms of movies scenes or songs. Far from simply being a form of entertainment, the best art arranges symbols, words, and ideas in ways that inspire and educate us. Bear with me then, as I take you on a journey to explore the larger themes in the famous musical, "The Wizard of Oz."

Problems Facing Our Youth

If I asked a room of people to list the problems facing our youth, most could easily do so. These are some of the common responses to my question:

• Teenage Pregnancy and Promiscuity

• Violence/Gangs

- Incarceration

- Lack of internal/external respect

- Using/Selling Drugs

- Poor School Performance/Dropping Out

- Little connection to history and culture

- Lack of motivation and initiative

- Easily influenced

Many of us know the *whats*, but we must have serious discussions around the *whys* and *hows*. In this article, I will address the issue of how we can understand and change the attitudes and behaviors of our youth, and I will use the famous "Wizard of Oz" movie as my primary reference. I know you might believe I am crazy, but again, just bear with me.

Let me begin by suggesting that this is not your typical children's movie. "Oz" contains symbols, actions, and truths we can use to understand the problems our youth face in society. Several years have passed since some of you viewed this movie, so we will begin with a summary of the characters and plot:

Summary of Movie

- Dorothy (the main character) finds herself in a new and strange place far away from her home

• She meets up with three main characters who like her, have a conflict

• They are told to follow the yellow-brick road to "Oz" where they will find the all-powerful and wise "Wonderful Wizard" who will solve their problems

• The "Wicked Witch of the West", threatened by their unity and quest for empowerment, sends several traps/obstacles their way to sabotage their progress

• They eventually meet the Wizard and the story concludes

Understanding the Characters & Their Problems

When we saw this movie as children, we probably did not appreciate many of the motifs and symbols presented. The four main characters in the "Wizard of Oz" have major problems or conflicts. Each character represents a type of person with a specific problem. Examine the following chart:

Person	*Problem*	*What problem Represents*
Dorothy	Away from home and can't get back	Being lost, confused, and disconnected from culture
The Scarecrow	Has no brain	Lack of intelligence and capability
The Lion	Has no courage	Low self-esteem, lack of confidence, failure to claim authority
The Tin Man	Has no heart	Being insensitive, lacking compassion and humanity

We can think of these characters as being types of people. One believes herself to be unintelligent, and not capable. Another lacks self-esteem and authority, and another is ruthless, heartless, and unfeeling. Sound familiar? When you add all these qualities together, you get Dorothy, a person that is LOST and disconnected. I submit that the problems we see in our young people stem from these same factors. They are victims of a society (and in some cases *parenting and educational systems*) that teach them they are not capable, not worthy, and destined for lives of failure. With thinking like this, we can understand why they display some of the symptoms we see, right?

Poppy Fields

The Wicked Witch of the **West** (get it?) observes the actions of our characters from a great distance. How can she do this? She uses a crystal ball, of course. Today's "wicked witches" use cameras, satellites, and surveillance devices. She does not like to see these characters unite and seek empowerment. Looking to sabotage their agenda, the witch sends them through a Poppy field, causing most of them to fall asleep.

But the question is, what is the significance of Poppy plants? Why do they cause some characters to sleep? What does this mean? Poppy plants are used to produce Heroin, Opium, and Morphine, three powerful narcotic drugs. Interesting when you consider how the government sent Black and Brown communities through similar "poppy fields" in the 60s, 70s and 80s. Just think about the Heroin, Cocaine, and Crack epidemics in our neighborhoods and all the organizations and families destroyed. The Wicked Witch of the West is alive and well it would appear....

About the "Wizard"

Our characters manage to stay together and overcome all the obstacles thrown their way. They finally meet the "Wonderful Wizard" who supposedly has the power to resolve each of their problems. The only problem is, he is a fake wizard. Quite simply, he is an ordinary white man using gadgets and propaganda to make himself seem all-powerful and superior...sound familiar?

Naturally, they are upset upon learning the wiz is a fake. They invested so much time, travel and energy to reach him. In fear of his life, and to pacify the people who are now ready to revolt, the Wizard gives them mere *symbols* of the intelligence, courage/leadership, heart/humanity they seek. At this point, we learn that they had the qualities they sought all along!

Interestingly, the "Wizard" gives them a diploma, medal, and award to symbolize the qualities they believe themselves lacking. Hence, two lies materialize. One, that they were deficient in the first place, and two, that they magically obtained certain qualities once the wizard validated them. See how this works?

Bringing It All Together

• This society and its institutions work to turn our youth into The Lion (no courage or self-esteem), The Scarecrow (no intelligence or capability), and The Tin Man (Insensitive, impolite, dangerous). When you add all of these qualities together, you have Dorothy (someone who is lost, confused, and disconnected from God and culture)

• Our youth are often steered into "poppy fields" to sabotage their progress (drugs, incarceration, gangs, dropping out of school, etc.)

• Our youth are taught to believe not in the authority of God, or themselves, but of men and women who set themselves up as gods

How Do We Resolve These Problems?

• Provide our children with a strong spiritual foundation so they do not bow to false gods, or wicked witches!

• Create opportunities for our children to develop a sense of <u>genuine and earned</u> achievement and accomplishment

• Imbue our children with knowledge of their ancestors, culture, and history ("There's no place like home")

• Teach character development. Our world is over-run by vain, arrogant, ignorant, and selfish people. We must raise children who are **useful, helpful and qualified**

• Teach our children to be leaders and problem-solvers, not followers and whiners; create opportunities for them to develop and utilize these skills

• Make education and self-improvement *non-negotiable and mandatory* in your household

• Connect them to good "witches," or mentors

• Do not set them up to fail by coddling them, failing to discipline them, or giving them undeserved gifts and awards

U.S. Crimes More Horrific Than Anything You've Seen on CSI

I once read a Huffington Post article entitled, "7 Places in your Home That Are Dirtier than Your Toilet."[23]

Who would have thought that the common cell phone has 500 times more bacteria, than a toilet, and a sponge 200,000 times more? Or that the average kitchen sink is dirtier than your *entire* bathroom? It turns out that our toilets are far more sanitary than many things we do

---

[23] http://www.huffingtonpost.com/2013/03/28/places-dirtier-than-your-toilet_n_2972129.html#slide=2276176

not see as threats to our health! One microbiologist suggested (do not try this at home) that it is safer for us to eat from our toilet seats than it is from our kitchen surfaces! And all this time, I believed my toilet was the dirtiest thing in my home.....

Before you scurry off to purchase carts of antibacterial wipes and sanitizing sprays, let us spend a minute reflecting on this information. *The thing we really believed to be filthy pales in comparison to the more dangerous and unresolved filth around us....*

This got me to thinking about how we have been conditioned to identify "filth" in our society like violent crime for example. Popular crime shows like *Law and Order*, everything on the ID Channel, or *CSI*, make us understand serial killings, abductions, rape and torture as acts of psychotic and sick individuals. Corporate-owned TV news programs contribute to this hysteria with their persistent reporting of seemingly isolated acts of brutality by sick and desperate citizens.

We watch these news reports in horror, some of us wishing the death penalty, life imprisonment, or an old-fashioned beating for the perpetrators of these horrible crimes

However, what if I told you that the U.S. government regularly has and continues to commit crimes more wicked and egregious than anything you have seen on the news or forensic crime shows? Let us examine this further:

1.   Deliberately   failing   schools:
In the midst of Ivy League and corporate-funded school reforms along with the increasing creation of charter schools, the intentional dumbing down of our children continues. Millions of young people cannot adequately read, write, speak, critically think or lead. Black and Brown children remain the disproportionate victims, almost securing their place as a permanent underclass. We were taught that education was supposed to eventually eliminate societal gaps. Instead, *the education industry reinforces them.* Moreover, this occurs within one of the world's richest and most educated nations.

2. Unfair and inhumane incarceration: With over 2 million inmates, America has the largest rate of incarceration among industrialized nations in the world. Approximately 760 of every 100,000 people are incarcerated in the United States. In comparison, Japan has 63, Germany 90, South Korea 97, and Britain 153 people incarcerated per 100,000. Furthermore, United States imprisonment has clear racial disparities. People of color constitute 60% of the inmate population; Black offenders often receive longer sentences for the same offences than their white counterparts; Black and Latino youth receive harsher punishment than white students and are arrested 70% more than white youth for school-related offenses. As Legal scholar Michelle Alexander notes, incarceration has become a new form of Jim Crow for Black people. When we combine this fact with the atrocious conditions inmates face, or the numbers of wrongly convicted inmates, this stands as a crime of tremendous magnitude.

3. **Imperialist Wars:** Conventionally, nations go to war when attacked by other nations. Nations conduct Imperialist wars to create or expand their empires by controlling the labor, trade, politics or

natural resources of another nation. This often involves declarations of war and/or establishing military bases in other countries. America's imperialist activities abroad are infamous, from the Spanish-American War in 1898 to Korea, Vietnam, the Gulf War and continuing military aggression in Afghanistan (not to mention scores of military interventions in several other countries). Excluding civilians, the U.S. military has killed over 10 million people around the world since WWII! Surprisingly we never describe such immoral and murderous actions as "serial killings" but this record of genocide far exceeds the murders committed by Ted Bundy, David Berkovitz, John Wayne Gacy, or Jeffrey Dahmer. In addition, The U.S. operates over 1000 military bases throughout the world, unfairly affecting the trade and political affairs of sovereign nations.

4. **Police brutality:** Police are sworn to serve and protect. Sometimes citizens benefit; usually businesses and rich people do. Far too often the very citizens whose taxes pay police salaries find themselves unfairly brutalized and murdered by police all over the country. Interestingly, we rarely hear of such attacks against white people. However, Blacks and Latinos have come to expect police brutality along with guilty police receiving exoneration from the courts. In some cases, these brutes have displayed sexual deviance and sadistic behaviour of certified serial killers.

5. **Poverty & its Consequences:** Due to corporate greed and the very mechanics of capitalism itself, America kills millions of people and tortures even more through poverty. Nearly 50 million people have no medical insurance and cannot pay the exorbitant fees for their medicine; almost 15% of American households seriously struggle

to eat regularly; Almost 50 million people in America meet the criteria of living in poverty. This is the largest amount since the poverty level was first established. The inability to generate a liveable wage or receive adequate medical or other forms of assistance leads to deaths from hunger and illness along with a tremendous number of homeless people. Somehow, this problem escalates regardless of who the president is or what political party wields power. This problem would be horrific by itself, but to occur in such a rich nation that spends so much money in defense and in aid to other nations is unacceptable and...criminal!

My simple point is that we cannot allow the corporate-controlled media to define crime for us or make us abhor the crimes of individual citizens while ignoring those government agencies commit on an institutional level. We cannot excuse heinous acts on the individual level for sure. It is equally unwise to excuse government acts that affect far more people in more compelling ways. In addition, if we call for the death penalty, lifetime imprisonment or psychiatric treatment for citizen-criminals, why do we allow institutional criminals whose actions affect far more people in far more devastating ways, to avoid accountability for their heinous acts? Is this a function of our ignorance, or our cowardice?

A Word About Black Cynics

You have seen their scowls, smirks, folded arms and indifferent eyes. You have observed their tendency to derail hope, passion and talk of change and social justice. This world, with its greed, dehumanizing manner, ruthless indifference and lust for domination, mass-produces them. I am referring to that population of people we call "cynics."

A "Cynic" is one who does not believe in the goodness or sincerity of people's motives or intentions. The troubling thing is that cynics exist within the very community of Black people who claim to be progressive and about change. Curious, isn't it?

As an activist and one fighting to educate and improve conditions, I have dealt with many cynical folk over the years. You can easily identify cynics. They typically fly under the radar in times of apathy and idleness. They usually emerge in discussions involving hope, forward movement and social empowerment or justice. They often shoot down every proposed method or push for change without providing any alternative. We can summarize their classic attitude as follows:

- "That's just the way things are. They'll never change."

- "I don't trust anybody."

- "I used to be like you, but I got smart."

- "I've heard it all before."

- "Everybody is out for themselves."

- "I'm just worried about me and mine."

Such people (if you allow them) will cause you to suffer without fighting back. They will crush your dreams and suffocate your spirit. They will have you succumb to despair and hopelessness, or make you feel powerless in the face of conflict. For these reasons, cynics represent the polar opposites of activists.

All social activists operate from the premise that economic, political, or social injustices are problems that *can and must be confronted by the people most experiencing them.* Beneath all of the rhetoric and activism lies a belief that "We the people" CAN organize research, confront and ultimately resolve problems or improve conditions. In other words, authentic organizers, leaders, and activists possess that most powerful of shields and weapons called **HOPE**. We also possess the **COURAGE** to stand up and speak out against social vices and oppression. Dick Gregory accurately summarized this when he noted, *"A leader for Black people must be like a turtle: tender on the inside, hard on the outside, and willing to stick their neck out."*

Cynics scoff at such people calling them idealistic, overly optimistic or suffering from "Martyr's Syndrome." They insist that oppressive systems and the individuals running them are all-powerful or at least richer, more intelligent and more committed than we. On top of this, they argue, "We the people" (particularly those with melanin) refuse to organize, are self-absorbed, materialistic, and plagued with division and discord. Such statements sting because they bear elements of truth we cannot overlook.

Yet, Black cynics seem to suffer from severe bouts of historical or political amnesia. They forget for example, how enslaved and largely illiterate Africans still managed to create their own schools. Memories of how free and enslaved Black folk fought physically and politically in the 19th century via civil war, plantation revolts, the underground railroad, establishment of Maroon societies, and the Abolitionist Movement to end Black bondage. Forgotten as well is how our people organized to challenge and dismantle legalized Apartheid (Jim Crow) in this nation, waging nonviolent war in the courts and in the streets against powerful and belligerent opposition.

Black cynics also suffer from short-term memory loss. Somehow, they forget or are unaware of the Black Power Movement, Black Arts Movement, and Anti-war or Free Speech Movements led by ordinary and extraordinary Black students, teachers, musicians, intellectuals and others just 5 decades ago.

The moral of this story, per examination of our history, is that we have made significant degrees of progress and have resisted our oppression at every step along the way and in every historical period using various tools, ideas and methods. While we are justified to perceive government bodies and officials with cynicism, we cannot afford to turn this inward on ourselves without serving the interests of our oppressors and causing incalculable damage to our instincts for freedom and justice.

History in other words, even when we account for all the broken promises, in fighting, and remnants of injustice still present, proves all of the cynics WRONG.

So the next time you have a discussion with a cynical brother or sister, listen to them, debate them if you choose, but NEVER internalize his or her defeatist or apathetic attitude. Recognize that they too, enjoy benefits, privileges and rights secured by Black people who dared to dream, and dared to visualize and fight for better conditions for themselves and their posterity.

Our story has always been one of people who defied the odds, conquered giants, and survived every obstacle our enemies devised for us. Our story is one of faith, hope, Vision, and work despite opposition. If 2000 years from now Black people no longer existed, and someone told our story, people would assume it was a tall-tale or myth. With all of our flaws and contradictions, WE ARE A MIRACULOUS PEOPLE CAPABLE OF MAKING MIRACLES OCCUR, AND LET NO ONE TELL YOU DIFFERENTLY.

PART II

"CLEAN UP"
Identifying and becoming critical of our own self-defeating ideas and behaviors individually and collectively, then correcting them

Are Reactionary "Conscious" Folk The New Black Sellouts?

When we typically think of the term "sellout", our brains rapidly flip through pictures or memories of media-celebrated Black folk that support ultra conservative, right-wing policies. These typically include: eliminating effective Affirmative Action initiatives, scapegoating poor Black people, attempting to reduce or eliminate public assistance, supporting increased U.S. military presence and actions abroad, defending or trivializing the epidemic of police brutality against Black bodies, insisting either that racism no longer exists or that fellow Black folk largely exaggerate its existence.

We view such individuals negatively and for good reason: the positions they take and the policies they support promote Black criminalization, defend and justify racist thought and practice, attack measures designed to stimulate relief or social equality, and dismiss/disregard legitimate Black suffering and grievances. In their opinion, we overly sensitive Black folk are too eager to accept handouts, and too lazy or pathological to exhibit the character and motivation needed to resolve problems we cause in the first place. They add a dose of patriotism to support their false claims, proudly describing the United States as a nation where "everyone can rise if they just work hard enough and exhibit personal responsibility."

But these misguided individuals are not our only collective problem. I have noticed a very disturbing trend manifest itself on city streets and reach viral proportions on social media. This is not a particularly new trend, but it has, in my opinion, become more pronounced and influential in the last few years. I am referring to (drum roll please) .... The shocking trend of *Black politically conscious folks (often self-proclaimed followers of Marcus Garvey and Malcolm X) taking reactionary and counter-revolutionary positions* that actually benefit the architects, beneficiaries, and practitioners of white supremacy!

Because their ideas and teachings make Black people more vulnerable to victimization and because they threaten to set the Black Liberation Movement backwards, one wonders if such people represent a new breed of (unintended) Black sellouts. This article will identify some of these curious positions or practices, and explain how each works to the advantage of white supremacists rather than the Black masses whom they are supposed to benefit.

I humbly suggest that we attempt to educate such folk to their complicity in our oppression, and if need be, **expose them** in an effort to neutralize their deliberate or unconscious sabotage of an entire people and liberation movement.

Patriarchy: Sexism or the oppression of our sisters is unacceptable and backwards. How do we justify fighting oppression outside of our community, yet reinforce it within our homes, organizations, and communities? Our liberation movement cannot substitute one form of exploitation for another, nor limit or attempt to proscribe the strength, leadership, and development of our sisters. Suggesting that Black women only play traditional (male-defined roles), that their grievances are invalid, or that they are to blame for eroding Black family values and wayward youth is blatantly sexist. What nation do we build, what enemy do we vanquish, what empowered communities do we create when we oppress or muzzle one-half of our population?

Taking positions that reinforce divisiveness, in fighting and domination only serve the interests of those who divide and conquer us already. This has no place in the thoughts or actions of a conscious Black person. Black girls and women have traditionally been the unsung sheroes in our history, providing on-the-ground labor, education, activism, and leadership, yet standing in the shadows of Black men, due to religious or biological fallacies we inherited from our oppressors.

Then we have "conscious" Black men who routinely beat sisters behind closed doors and have the audacity to justify such actions by quoting "king of the castle," or "Head of the household" logic. Our **entire** community must be healed, empowered, and primed for success, not just men. Valid critiques of feminist ideology are necessary and important. Complete disregard of sisters' voice, experiences and value however, is unacceptable.

Using violence against other Black folk with whom we disagree. We know from the days of Cointelpro under Hoover's leadership, that the enemy used divide and conquer tactics to arouse resentment and acts of violence between Nationalist groups. Killing ourselves in this fashion clearly works to the advantage of those who want to neutralize radical Black resistance. No responsible, well-studied or disciplined individual would ever resort to such actions. In this era however, this is highly possible given the bravado and rigid dogma of certain groups. We must learn to mediate our conflicts nonviolently.

Assuming unqualified authority: While it is true that everyone has opinions and the right to express them, it is *equally true that* not all opinions are valid. Valid opinions, positions, or theories are those supported with fact, experience, and sound analysis.

The rise of the internet and social media now provides anyone with a free platform to share his/her ideas or theories with people all over the world. As one does this, they gain "friends" or followers. This may give someone the false impression that his or her popularity equates to authority or legitimacy. However, if the person in question hasn't paid their dues (i.e. established credibility in the community, created a quality body of work, participated in activism, writing, institution-building, leading, community organizations/political struggle, educating and solving problems, study and research, etc.), they are not *qualified* to speak with authority or give grand proclamations on these issues.

Any person who sincerely wants to represent, lead, advance or help to organize Black people should love and respect us enough to render *quality* service and take the time to *adequately prepare* themselves to do so. In addition, we should be *deeply suspicious* of those who do not. As I posted on Facebook,

"I believe it's important and necessary to welcome advice or opinion. Ultimately, I tend to trust and respect the advice/opinions of people who have demonstrated success or accomplishment regarding the topic in question. Informed opinions hold more weight, are usually more relevant and more helpful to me. I would appreciate both perspectives on escaping slavery, but would take Harriet Tubman's advice more seriously than that of someone who did not participate in liberating African people. Harriet make 19 successful liberation trips and helped over 3000 slaves escape to their freedom within a ten-year period!

You get the point, I'm sure. Be very careful of people that want acclaim or recognition or who have much to say, but have not qualified themselves through study, experience and accomplishment. This is a sure recipe for DISASTER. Always we must ask, what have you done? What are you doing? What are you working on now? There are many "false prophets" so to speak."

Moreover, people that truly feel strongly about social and political issues should demonstrate this by being involved in these issues beyond simple Facebook and Twitter posts. If you decry miseducation of our youth, do not let your activism end with a social media post. Become a teacher, create a school or afterschool program, or create an organization to challenge the public school system. If you feel strongly about Black Liberation, become meaningfully involved and engaged." In another social media post I noted, *"The next time someone pontificates about injustice, miseducation, poverty, violence or any other social vice, ask them the million dollar question: What have you done and what are you doing about it? We have more than enough commentators and cheerleaders. What we need are more players and coaches!"* My position on this subject should not be misinterpreted as elitism. One need not be a college graduate, expert on a subject, or have a certain income level to be meaningfully involved and engaged. Our history is replete with examples of informally educated, non-celebrity, and/or poor people whose conviction and courage led them to educate, organize, build institutions, and participate in liberation movements.

Lack of critical thinking/analysis: There is a disturbing trend of anti-intellectualism within some elements of the Black "conscious community." We simply cannot effectively dismantle white supremacy if we do not study the forces/individuals behind it and their methods. We cannot responsibly ask people to join our cause or organization without explaining to them how and why they are oppressed, who is responsible for their subjugation, and what we can do about it. Pronouncements and declarations are not enough; we must develop an accurate analysis of white supremacy and how it operates, then be able to communicate that effectively to members of our community, then organize our people and provide them with inspiration and tools to overthrow the devils internally and externally. All of our most effective and revered leaders and activists understood this including (but not limited to) Marcus Garvey, Elijah Muhammad, Dr. King, Ella Baker, Kwame Ture, Kwame Nkrumah, Malcolm X, and so on. All understood that our people must know how societal systems work to keep us powerless and divided. This - along with developing an empowering knowledge of self - is the foundation to developing political consciousness. There is no way around it...we must study and know our enemy, how he thinks, operates, and where he is weak. Read "The Art of War," observe how athletes view film of their opponents. Why then, would some in the conscious community ignore such a pivotal element of liberation? Sound analysis requires serious and sustained study. Some simply don't want to do this tedious and unglamorous work. It is much easier to simply make authoritative proclamations or give the community orders without sufficient context or substance. The other reason for this I suspect, is that some of these overnight commentators are in fact, agents, informers and provocateurs working to mislead, disrupt, and sabotage radical Black movement. Being well-informed and analytical doesn't mean that we become paralyzed in abstract discussions of "the white man." We still need to eliminate certain behaviors in our own community, build our own institutions, and develop harmony and solidarity. No matter how much we may choose to ignore agents and systems of white supremacy, they definitely do not ignore us! To the contrary, they study our loyalties, music, family structure, spending habits, and political and cultural influences thoroughly. Moreover, this partly explains why they are so effective in subjugating our communities and organizations! Does anyone remember Cointelpro? **Footnote**

Black Liberation is not a leisurely game of pool, or some ego-driven contest for bragging rights. This is a movement whose key objectives include our safety, empowered lives, liberty, progress, and a promising future for our children. Play Chess, not checkers, Black people! Listen and observe closely. Make moves that are strategic. Discard opinions/positions if you realize they are reactionary or do not hold weight. Ask, "Who does my political positions benefit or challenge?" If we fail to do this, some of us who presumably work to advance Black people, might actually be doing more to advance our enemies' interests than our own. And this - whether done intentionally or not - might just comprise a new (and deeply ironic) form of **selling-out.**

Let's Work Together: We Need a Black United Front!

If you have followed my recent articles on internal challenges and the call to organize, you will notice that I am laying a framework for effective leadership and organizing. This is so important because Black people are still largely oppressed, impoverished, and suffering despite having more Black politicians, education and technology than at any previous time in our history.

Indeed, these are curious times. 90% of our news/information is controlled by 6 mega-corporations, the United States government passed legislation to monitor internet activity and share users' personal information, and police brutality is at an all-time high.[24] Add to this the chronic failure of our public schools to teach Black students, and a **prison system** that disproportionately affects Black, Brown, and poor people, and you have explored *just the tip of the iceberg* concerning the problems confronting us in America.

Yet in face of these blatantly oppressive conditions some of our "leaders" in typical house Negro fashion, continue to sell us the same tired set of patriotic American commandments: "Go to school," "work hard," "pray," "vote in national elections," and "trust the system to do its job." Most of these approaches fail to seriously challenge these systems and only work for a *select minority of us*. Meanwhile, the mainstream religious, political, and educational institutions play their parts in selling and justifying such nonsense, and we good citizens go along with it even though our lived experiences tell us *such thinking/practices haven't worked in the past, and do not work now,* at least not for the majority of us.

Complicating matters is the unfortunate reality that many of us that do know/understand the situation are unwilling to organize with the people and implement our various theories, philosophies, and methods. And far too many of us allow artificial divisions, titles, ideologies, and denominations to get in the way.

---

[24] Refer to the Malcolm X Grassroots Movement's report *"Operation Ghetto Storm: Annual Report on the Extrajudicial Killing of Black People by Police, Security Guards and Vigilantes."*

Based on Black history and culture (or at least my understanding of them) our diversity is not a curse, but a blessing. It insures that we have a deep and broad ocean of resources and perspectives to draw from. Our churches for example always contained people with a variety of talents, ideas and interpretations, and the same is true for our Masonic lodges, community organizations and civic organizations. The only groups within our communities in which all members are identical in belief and practice are *cults*, which by definition largely cater to their own members rather than the masses. When dealing with a 10-headed monster like white supremacy, we must have the capacity and flexibility of a large and diverse arsenal to defeat it. One type of approach simply will not be effective.

Brother Malcolm X skilfully advocated for a Black united front approach of organizing in his famous "Message to the Grassroots" speech. Drawing inspiration from the Bandung Conference of 1955 (in which 29 Asian and African nations met to develop a strategy to combat colonialism), he urged Black people to become less territorial and to think in terms of a **Black United Front.**

Today, we recognize that our battle includes an analysis of gender, class, and imperialism in addition to race and that oppression is more sophisticated today then when Malcolm lived. The problems we face today cannot be solved simply by "excluding the white man" for we now know that we cannot determine a person's politics simply using the rubric of race. We have people of color (i.e. Ward Connerly, Larry Elder) whose thinking and behavior join them with the enemy, and whites (i.e. Tim Wise) who are progressive and serious about social change. Yet, Malcolm's words concerning the formation of a Black united front remain relevant. We can delude ourselves into thinking we will win this war with unilateral leadership, cults, or an organization of identical thinkers and activists. However, how practical is this approach in a Black community composed of feminists, socialists, nationalists, religious and atheist folk? How do we win a battle with less than one-half of 1% of our people represented and participating or at least sympathetic to the cause?

The days of believing only one organization, idea, or method would save us are dead and gone. That approach only heightens our division, helps the enemy conquer us, promotes rivalry/fratricide and leads to disjointed and disconnected efforts (Study the forces that weakened Garvey's brilliant movement). What we need is a Black organization that works with other organizations to get things done, rather than arguing among ourselves over differences and accomplishing nothing.

The key words for today are collaboration and grassroots organizing. How is it possible to organize people with such a diversity of beliefs? Just as Malcolm noted, by identifying points of common interest and working together around them. All of our people need to eat, earn income, have shelter, healthcare, legal representation if necessary, adequate education/training, and be protected from brutality and discriminatory practices, right? Therefore, we form organizations and work with existing organizations to address these issues, bringing all of our diverse ideas, methods, talents, and resources to the table.

This idea of a united front is neither new nor abstract. We have tangible precedents for this in the Bandung Conference, the African Union, and the National Black United Front. When we organize in this manner, a strange thing happens: We begin to form relationships and mutual respect for each other despite our differences, and we have multiple resources and people on our team!

I am working with other progressive-minded Black folks to create this type of grassroots Black organization as you read this.[25] We must resist the propaganda that Black folks cannot organize or that all of us must believe the same thing. Aren't you tired of complaining about the issues, fighting over petty distinctions and continuing to suffer? Don't you believe in our right to be free and empowered and our need to work together to make this happen? The doors of self-reliance, collaborative leadership, and social justice/political empowerment are open. Who will **come**?

---

[25] **"Souljahs of the People."** https://truself143.wix.com/souljahz

"Gangsta" is not Revolutionary!

In 1963 Brother Malcolm X once famously warned, "If some of you understood what a revolution really is, you wouldn't use the word. Revolution is bloody, revolution is hostile, revolution destroys everything in its way." [26]

I have reason to believe that many politically minded college students, hip-hop artists, and other members of our community, mistakenly refer to themselves as "revolutionary" because they confuse the term's meaning.

---

[26] Malcolm X, "*Message to the Grassroots in America*." Northern Negro Grass Roots Leadership Conference, Detroit, MI, November 10, 1963.

One problem we face in discussing anything revolutionary is that the term and its implications are not fully understood. Naturally, this society's elite benefit from our confusion in this regard. They have no interest in losing their power or prestige, and maintaining confusion within potential rebel forces helps to maintain power arrangements while compromising revolutionary activity.

Language, which provides us with definition, clarity, and therefore direction, is a key tool used to misdirect our liberation movements. Many of us in the Hip Hop and conscious community facilitate our own confusion when we take words and change them to suit our interests.

For example, our word "gangsta" evolves from the word "gangster." A gangster is a thug who uses any means necessary to enrich himself. A gangster by definition is selfish and territorial; they operate from the vantage point of securing and empowering themselves, their turf, and their "gang" only. For these reasons, gangs (unless properly politicised) are reactionary and go against community interests by definition.

Interestingly, gangsters (and wannabees) portray themselves as being anti-establishment but in reality, they mirror the values of our governing bodies. Self-serving violence, capitalist expansion, profit-obsession, repression of dissenting voices/ideas, and control of territory are key qualities of the United States government.

In similar fashion, gangsters are infatuated with the idea of capitalist expansion, creating and controlling new markets (using intimidation and coercion), and creating a stream of infinite profits regardless of the people injured, impoverished or killed as a result. Like the government, gangs seize and control territory, suppress freedom of expression, and use violence to impose their will upon those weaker and less organized than themselves. Contrary to popular opinion, gangsters do not oppose the status quo; they actually support it. The only difference is that they do so without the "legitimate" or legal protection of the state.

What is it then that we common folk find so attractive about gangsters? Certainly, their general disregard for rules, law enforcement agencies, and societal norms fascinates us; they do things most of us are too fearful or powerless to do. A member of La Cosa Nostra (the Mafia) for example, enacts his/her own form of retribution against violators, rather than trusting the flawed criminal justice system to do so.

The Bloods or Crips do not write grants to federal and private agencies for money to secure their needs. They do not sell candy, have bake sales or host traditional fundraising events. They steal or extort the money they need from others or sell drugs (in their community) to procure it. Street gangs do not petition the police department to protect their territory; they use organized and militarised power to do it themselves.

Their proactive stances, high level of organization, willingness and ability to protect and provide for their own, and refusal to place trust in societal institutions is, well, attractive to we Black folk in the civilian population.

This explains the continuing romance the American public has with gangster movies and the tendency for so many rap artists to name themselves after iconic gangsters (or in Jim Jones' case, psychotic cult leaders).

Some Black organizations active in the Black Power Movement astutely recognized the political potential existent within local street gangs or criminal elements and attempted to recruit, reform and absorb them into the revolutionary fold (the Black Panther Party immediately comes to mind in this regard).

In some cases, this strategy produced limited success. Typically, though, the gangster element responded mostly to the paramilitary appeal of the Panthers for example, rather than their call to political and community organizing work.[27] In addition, gang members often continued their criminal activities as members or allies of the recruiting organization.

For example, the "Philadelphia Black Mafia" continued to distribute heroin, perform murders for hire, and extort other drug dealers in the 1970s, even as official members in the Nation of Islam's Temple #12.[28] The Black Panthers in Chicago attempted to form an alliance with the Blackstone Rangers - also known as the Black P. Stone Nation or El Rukins, a politically minded street organization with earlier gang roots. The Rangers were heavily influenced by Black Nationalist Islam and the Moorish Science Temple, but became

---

[27] Kathleen Cleaver and George Katsiaficas. "Liberation, Imagination and the Black Panther Party: A New Look at the Black Panthers and their Legacy," p.134 Routledge: NY, 2001.

[28] Griffin, Sean. Philadelphia's Black Mafia: A Social and Political History. Kluwer Academic Publishers, 2003.

dismantled due to the FBI and CointelPro, internal leadership rivalry and continued criminal activity.[29]

Whatever our romance with the gangster lifestyle may be, the fact remains that embodying a criminal lifestyle, exhibiting predatory behavior, and becoming rich and powerful from these activities, does not make one a revolutionary. One is not a revolutionary unless his/her motivations and actions benefit and positively transform the thnking/behavior of the masses, while challenging/dismantling systems of oppression. While all human beings are capable of redemption or political transformation (as we saw with Malcolm X or more recently with our outstanding Detroit-based organizer and "Souljahs of the People"[30] co-founder Yusef Bunchy Shakur) reforming the gangster element is far more difficult and developmental than we realize. It is difficult for a person to abandon predatory behavior they have embraced for several years and behavior that brings them status and wealth. Unless we provide financial incentives greater than those provided by street life, and truly transform our gang-affiliated brethren from community predators to community servants, our efforts in this regard will continue to be compromised.

---

[29] Lance Williams, "The Black Pyramid Stone: Black Power, Politics, and Gangbanging," University of Illinois at Chicago School of Public Health, February 12, 2001 Transcription:
http://www.uic.edu/orgs/kbc/ganghistory/UrbanCrisis/Blackstone/lance.htm

[30] http://truself143.wix.com/souljahz

Why Gangsters are not Revolutionary

It is both inaccurate and irresponsible to confuse being "gangsta" with being revolutionary. Perhaps we need a redefinition of terms. A revolutionary seeks total liberation of the people from all forms of ignorance, and oppression. A revolutionary seeks humane treatment for his/her people and has no tolerance for discrimination on any basis. A revolutionary seeks to expose and eliminate elitist and brutal authorities.

When we approach the conversation from this perspective, we realize that gangstas are not revolutionary, but conflicted reactionaries. They have internalized the false teachings of their societal masters, leading them to hate themselves, devalue and abuse women, disregard family responsibilities, and personify in every conceivable way the most vicious white supremacist roles and perceptions of Black people.

A conflicted reactionary will read and quote Malcolm X and Marcus Garvey, call for Black solidarity, yet go out and sell drugs in their community, extort Black businesses, create prostitution rings composed of Black girls, and become loan sharks to desperate and impoverished working-class Black civilians, while justifying these actions as "attempts to eat and survive." This contradiction magnifies when we observe that such folks only brutalize, degrade, rob, and exploit one group of people...his/her own!

Some in the "Revolutionary But Gangsta" (RBG) Movement attempt to fuse the gangsta persona with that of a revolutionary. What results are profanity-laced, bitter accusations (or acts of violence) against those critical of them; misogynist and patriarchal views and practices; predatory actions and attitudes toward their home communities. There is no role for gangsterism in revolutionary practice. In fact, revolutionaries often attempt to transform the lumpen-proletariat in our communities, and often to no avail.

The Malcolm X Grassroots Movement published a report[31] last year suggesting that a Black or Latino person is killed or physically attacked every 36 hours by a law enforcement agent or white vigilante. This report speaks to a very clear need for urban communities to organize and protect themselves from racial violence. Yet the very people most prepared and able to play this role consistently refuse to patrol Black communities, monitor police activity and intervene on behalf of their violated brothers and sisters. In Chicago, and many urban centers around this country, Black and Latino gangsters prey on their own people. However, when it comes time to put an end to police brutality, these gangsters are conspicuously absent and silent.

Keeping it "real"

A key challenge for us is to be clear on the terms we use, our motivations, and to make sure our actions correspond with our theories. We cannot romanticize gangsterism in our communities. As

---

[31] *Malcolm X Grassroots Movement, "Operation Ghetto Storm: 2012 Annual Report on the Extrajudicial Killing of 313 Black People."*

Minister Farrakhan says, "God didn't make you thugs and hoes....the white man did." We must teach our youth that the ugliness, disrespect, violence, and misogyny they exhibit are in fact, reflections of how other people view us. We must teach them how such actions benefit those who exploit and mistreat us.

While many valiant Black activists and organizations have facilitated gang truces, this is not enough. We must begin a long-term process of truly politically educating our criminal elements and raising their consciousness. We must help them understand the diabolical role they play in subjugating our people and empowering for example, the prison industrial complex and consequently, their own neo-enslavement.

Our continued failure to make the distinction between being revolutionary versus reactionary serves the interests of oppressive societal forces while betraying community interests. Think about it....whose interests are served when we adopt language and behavior that alienates our family members, creates dysfunctional relationships, increases Black/Latino incarceration and murder rates, encourages disrespect for learning, and perpetuates cycles of ugly in-fighting within our community? What we need to understand is that Black street gangs as we know them today began in urban areas after this government destroyed our Black Nationalist organizations. Gangs filled in the void left by all the warriors killed, imprisoned, or missing in action. Some began with noble community development intentions, but soon became reactionary.

View the documentary *"Bastards of the Party"*[32] when you can. Think about how drugs, violence, and other gang activities corrode our communities throughout the United States. Then ask yourselves: "Do we want to serve the interests of those who despise and mistreat us, or do we want to be active agents of our own liberation?" There is no room for ambiguity on this issue. You can choose to be a revolutionary, or a gangster, but you cannot be both...

----

[32] Antoine Fuqua, Cle Sloan. (2005). *Bastards of the Party*. United States. View the entire documentary at https://goo.gl/nvnBOK.

Enough of the Feel-Good Black History!

Historical approaches, like most other things, change over time. Of course, history itself (past events, activities and individual expression) does not change, but the manner in which we interpret it, our aim in researching it, or the manner in which we use it, inevitably does. This article explores the relevance of Black historical research and will provide a critique of what I call "Feel Good" or simplified Black history.

In scholarly circles, we refer to the study of how history is conducted, written and interpreted as "historiography." If you follow the historiography of Black or African-American Studies, you will notice that it has changed over time. Early pioneers of the field like J.A. Rogers, concerned themselves with "contributionist" or "vindicationist" Black history that focused on proving our worth and humanity through listing important Black figures, significant dates and African/Black contributions to world civilization.

During the 19th and early 20th centuries, this emphasis on Black contributions to humanity was necessary because white society constantly spread the propaganda that Black people "Were nothing, had nothing, and contributed nothing." The "First Black to do this," or "Did you know" type of Black history was crucial and relevant in years past, because we had to challenge myths of Black inferiority and incompetence to whites, while resurrecting the crushed spirits and psyches of our own people.

Racism and anti-Black sentiment still exists. However, as times and needs change, so does historiography. It is safe to conclude that the majority of Black children, youth and adults today know something about Black intelligence, accomplishment and pride. This is an important and lasting harvest of the Civil Rights and Black Power Movements. Today we are familiar (even if only in an elementary sense) with Harriet Tubman, Frederick Douglass, Martin Luther King Jr., even Malcolm X and Huey P. Newton. We know or at least have heard that "Black is beautiful." The election of Barrack Obama as the nation's first Black president and the media dominance of Oprah Winfrey are (at least symbolically) evidence of Black achievement and ability that no one can reasonably discount.

Therefore, in the 21st century, it is not enough to simply quote or highlight famous Black leaders, produce a list of Black "firsts", or cite Black trivia. **Doing so actually represents a digression or backwards step** since we already have tons of evidence and scholarship in this regard.

We live at a curious time where despite the presence of a Black president, Black million and billionaires, thousands of Black elected officials, successful Black entrepreneurs, scientists, attorneys, professors, writers, and entertainers, WE ARE STILL OPPRESSED, MARGINALIZED AND MISTREATED. Our children don't receive the education they need in chronically low-performing public schools, police officers and white vigilantes still murder us with impunity, privatized U.S. prisons keep millions of us in captivity while exploiting our labor, most of us have no or very little assets, we die younger and more frequently than any other group in this country, and our rate of unemployment and underemployment is astronomical.

The evidence overwhelmingly suggests that we do not need feel-good history. Much of what passes for "Black history today (particularly on social media like Facebook) is oversimplified and obsolete. What we need right now and going forward are get-right, get-empowered, get-free Black Studies! Anything involving or affecting Black people should be under examination. Moreover, we must overcome our oversimplified definitions of history or relevant Black Studies.

This means we must change our concept of history from that of trivia, highlighting exceptional Black people, and emphasizing Black contributions. We need to seriously study the Black experience in all class dimensions, locations, religious and political contexts, in every sphere of our existence, and the manner in which these experiences affect us. We must do this earnestly and in a critical manner with an aim of better understanding the problems we face, and resolving or correcting them. For example, the following constitute just a few of the important issues that history can help us intelligently address:

- Past mistakes, we should avoid today.

- Uncovering new aspects of important leaders/organizations and re-appraising their significance, limitations, and contributions.

- Creating and evaluating organizations or effective blueprints/programs for economic or political development.

- Important but under-represented issues and historical figures/movements that deserve more of our attention

- Black behaviors, ideas, attitudes and methods that we need to critique and either refine or eliminate.

No individual, organization, movement, or ideology is above critique. We need solutions, clarity, direction and answers in addition to studies that celebrate and affirm us. Simply put, feel-good Black history does not provide all of these dimensions. Too many of us are metaphorically riding donkeys when we should be exploring space. Too many of us metaphorically use Morse code in an era of laptops, tablets, smartphones and the internet. Let's get our heads out of the sand and engage in studies of our experience that are useful and relevant to our condition, because being liberated and empowered is the one sure way to actually "feel good."

Ideological Flaws in the Conscious Community

I am convinced that some of our greatest internal barriers to progress come from misguided ideologies promoted by some members of what we have come to know as the "Conscious community." People that are politically or socially conscious are presumed to be in touch with the problems, resources, history and needs of the Black community. Such people and groups also develop ideologies which they believe effectively address and solve the problems we face. However, ideologies are not perfect, and some are actually overly simplified, impractical, disconnected from the political or economic realities we face, or largely ineffective.

This article will address ultra-conservative and fundamentalist folk whose ideologies need serious re-examination.

People, like organizations and ideologies are works in progress. Therefore, we should expect our opinions, solutions and analysis to be imperfect, and we should constantly work to rework and refine them based on the socio-political context in which we live.

Conservative Black Nationalists for example, naively think that simply amassing material wealth, businesses and land (Black capitalism) will end our oppression or go unchallenged by the white corporate authorities. It's as if such people do not know that Black people have established all-Black, economically vigorous communities in America before that were ultimately destroyed by jealous and racist whites. From 1863 to 1919 for example, eight successful Black communities in the United States were ultimately destroyed by violent white mobs. These communities existed in New York City, Atlanta, Tulsa, Chicago, Rosewood, St. Louis, Knoxville, and Washington, D.C.

The conservative Nationalists also fail to hold systemic forces of oppression accountable because they are too busy blaming Black people for every ounce of their suffering and dysfunction. Advocates of these ideas subtly hate and resent the very people they claim to represent and often take positions and support policies very similar to those of our enemies, rendering them useless to us. This group will turn us into a nation of middle class apologists for oppression who accommodate to oppressive forces rather than challenging them.

The second group I will call "fundamentalist nationalists." Such advocates have almost no gender or class analysis. The only issue they identify is race. This group has a tendency to become violent with those people who disagree, they fail to understand forms of struggle that don't involve armed revolt, and they often adopt an oversimplified "with us or against us" type of reasoning. This group idea isolates Black members of the LGBT community, women, and members of the Black religious community. In addition, they often fail to address the complexity of our problems, focus solely on armed revolution and separation without considering practical short-range solutions and programs.

This phrase "Conscious Community" is quite popular these days. I use it myself. It refers to those brothers and sisters with some useful degree of sociopolitical awareness, African-centered knowledge of Black history or the Black experience, and an understanding of white supremacy. In an ideal world, this term also describes people who fuse their knowledge and understanding of such things with programs, institutions, activism, and things designed to help Black people Wake up, Clean up, and Stand up! However as we all probably agree, this is not an ideal world, but a REAL world, and definitions of "conscious community" are as confused and varied as members of this community itself. Nevertheless, I will go with this term for now, as it is an all-embracing term with which most of us are familiar.

I want us to spend some time being critical of this community that includes Black artists, writers, intellectuals, activists, organizers, students, workers, and national organization leaders and their members. The simple yet uncomfortable truth is that some members of this community - a community I claim for myself as well - are becoming a large part of our collective problem rather than a reassuring a liberating part of the solution for Black folk seeking empowerment and liberation. Why is a serious critique of the Black conscious community warranted? Note the following compelling reasons:

- They/we sometimes attract huge followings and exert some degree of influence on these followers particularly their understanding of key concepts like identity, oppression, solidarity, and resistance.

- In some cases, they/we are responsible for monies and other resources solicited and collected from our community, for starting programs, institutions, and political movements.

- Because they/we tend to be more articulate, fearless, and knowledgeable than most, the masses of our community tend to see us as trustworthy leaders and molders of community consensus and empowerment.

- They/we play a major role in our people's capacity to "Wake up, Clean up, and Stand up."

Our people deserve the most sincere and committed individuals advocating on their behalf, raising consciousness, and cultivating Black resistance to oppression. While some clearly have an over-inflated sense of importance, members of this community **are** important for the reasons stated above, and then some. Because our integrity and the success of our efforts are so largely influenced by the conscious community, it is our duty to support those who speak, educate, organize and fight with us effectively.

However when such people are inaccurate, self-serving, or leading us in counterproductive directions or toward disastrous outcomes, we also have the duty to be **critical.** Neglecting to do so just because some individuals or organizations are popular, or even well intentioned, is not patriotic or righteous - It is cowardly, foolish and counter-revolutionary, period. As Dr. King reminded us,

Cowardice asks the question: is it safe? Expediency asks the question: is it political? Vanity asks the question: is it popular? But conscience asks the question: is it right? And there comes a time when one must take a position that is neither safe, nor political, nor popular - but one must take it simply because it is right.

With this guiding principle in mind, I offer the following ideas and practices that some members of the conscious community champion but are (in my opinion) fundamentally flawed and destined to set our movement backwards.

The belief that knocking on doors, and/or holding rallies, marches and protests are the only legitimate forms of protest. We are now over a decade into the 21st Century. This is an exciting time when internet technology, smartphones and social media make the world smaller and more manageable. This scenario radically improves our ability to conduct research and communicate. We simply cannot afford to stay in the Fred Flintstone era of activism. It is time to leave "Bedrock" behind and explore the world of the "Jetsons" that is upon us. We must continue the best practices of traditional activism while effectively utilizing the new tools at our disposal so that we can reach more people, and better expose, challenge, and defeat our enemies while empowering and liberating ourselves.

Another fact bears repeating: We must also realize that our enemies attack and oppress us in almost every major area of human activity and that they use multiple means to do so. We cannot successfully counter such a sophisticated multi-level attack by using one mode or weapon. If we members of the conscious community are serious about removing the shackles of ignorance and oppression, we need to recognize, support and participate in varied forms of consciousness-raising and resistance including but not limited to: blogging, social media, internet conferences, building alternative and African-centered institutions, in addition to using traditional forms of activism and education. White supremacy is a twenty-headed and twenty-hearted beast with body parts that regenerate themselves when damaged. We cannot defeat that beast with one sword or one tactic.

Degrading, insulting, and using unnecessarily crass and vulgar language, against fellow members of the conscious community with whom we disagree. I don't know when it became acceptable to demoralize and belittle other activists, intellectuals, leaders and community organizers simply because we disagree with their tactics or strategy. Elements of fundamentalist Nationalism exist among some members of the conscious community. This narrow-minded, dogmatic, intolerant, and simplistic mode of leadership/activism is dangerous and threatens to create violent and unproductive tribalism in our community. Fascism is NEVER fashionable. I find that many "conscious" people who claim to follow and respect Brother Malcolm, tend to behave this way. Malcolm himself behaved this way, insulting Dr. King and other Black leaders with whom he had ideological and tactical disagreements. He later recognized his mistake, and attempted to correct himself by apologizing publicly to those he insulted, and by attempting to work with civil rights leaders he believed were sincere. We cannot on one hand proclaim to our community that we need "all hands on deck," then on the other hand, insult and question the authenticity of those who have differing opinions or who participate in varied forms of activism. This of course, does not suggest we should allow opportunistic, self-serving Black collaborators of oppression to exist without challenge. To the contrary, we must challenge them vigorously.

There is room in the struggle for several organizations, perspectives and approaches. The only thing we absolutely cannot tolerate in any circumstance, are insincere and opportunistic types whose lust for fame, money or recognition compromise our forward movement, and government informants. We must learn to disagree with fellow conscious folk in a mature and responsible fashion, which allows us to still work together and share resources and networks down the road. We can all agree that life for those of us in the Black liberation struggle is often uncomfortable, lonely, and highly pressurized. We need support! Therefore, we should work on heightening movement morale, giving credit where due, promoting/supporting other people's activities, and building sustained and productive relationships with fellow activists, rather than insulting them

Failing to emphasize and promote universally empowering qualities/virtues of personal development. The conscious community famously emphasizes our need to be culturally and historically connected, appreciative of Africa's contributions to world civilization, and vigorous in exposing and challenging white supremacy. These are in my estimation, mandatory and pivotal to our collective development.

However, we cannot forget the equally important role of personal development. We compromise all efforts at collective empowerment if we fail to promote and model the qualities and virtues of being organized in thought and practice, embodying a strong work-ethic, striving for academic and general excellence in all we do, developing good character and exercising self-discipline.

These tools helped our ancestors to advance/develop themselves despite seemingly overwhelming societal oppression and persecution, and we do ourselves well to remember and emulate this. DuBois, Malcolm, and Ella Baker were not just dedicated opponents to white supremacy; they were also devout practitioners of personal empowerment, starting with themselves.

Do the research and observe their meticulous time management, tireless work ethic, and self-discipline. Do not allow ignorant people to deem these qualities "white" or counter-revolutionary. Realizing the importance of this point, I wrote a book entitled, *Truth for our Youth: A Self-Empowerment Book for Teens.*[33] This book teaches our youth how to manage time, make solid decisions, avoid societal traps develop self-love and confidence, and the importance of education and excellence. It is an important read for our teens, families and youth development workers.

---

[33] Find more information at http://goo.gl/58yX20.

Creating or promoting a climate of anti-intellectualism. Brother Malcolm wrote, *"Education is our passport to the future, for tomorrow belongs to those who prepare for it today."* If education (research, reading, studying, analyzing) give us the power and mobility to move forward and explore possibilities, then ignorance is our prison sentence of long-term solitary confinement allowing for isolation, deprivation, and the inability to exercise mobility and self-reliance.

If you did not obtain a college education, you can still read, study and be analytical. If you are college-educated, realize your education did not start nor will it end with earning a degree. However you acquire education, formally or informally, is your business... just make sure you ACQUIRE IT! Ignorant, misinformed people who are heavy on opinion and light on study do us little good. We need people who can not only consume, understand and explain information, but who can also create, publish and put information into practical use.

Not everyone will be an intellectual or scholar. Nor will everyone be a hardcore "boots-on-the-ground" activist. Our ancestors revered knowledge and respected those who possessed it. Somehow, we have gone backwards on this issue. People cannot **do** the right things unless they **know** the right things. We will also have to agree that the purpose of research and study is not simply to accumulate a bunch of facts or trivia, but to gain information and the ability to use that information to understand the world, past and current events, and to positively affect present and future circumstances. I am personally not impressed with people who can regurgitate tons of trivia. I am more concerned with uncovering meaning and analysis, and discovering ways to use that information meaningfully.

We should support our radical intellectuals and activists. Instead of arguing over who is most or least important, we should encourage mutual respect and cooperation. Activists should read the work of radical intellectuals (alive and deceased) in an effort to better refine their analysis of the sociopolitical terrain. End this nonsensical hatred of scholars, intellectuals, or the college-educated Black folk in our community.

If you've read or quoted Chancellor Williams, DuBois, Carter G. Woodson, Yosef Ben-Jochannan, John Henrik Clarke, Amos Wilson, Kwame Nkrumah, Huey P. Newton, Ella Baker, Stokely Carmichael, Khalid Muhammad, Sister Souljah, Frantz Fanon, Amilcar Cabral, Walter Rodney, Angela Davis, or Cheikh Anta Diop, you actively respect and utilize the work of college-educated Black folk with revolutionary credibility;

Likewise, if you admire Frederick Douglass, J.A. Rogers, Marcus Garvey, Elijah Muhammad, Patrice Lumumba, Malcolm X, Minister Farrakhan, Fannie Lou Hamer, Maya Angelou, or George Jackson, you appreciate self-taught organic Black intellectuals whose revolutionary credibility is also above reproach.

Patriarchy and Homophobia. Most conscious brothers and sisters speak out against racism, police brutality, miseducation, poverty, war, and a list of other social ills. Yet some of these same individuals insult and exclude Black women and Black members of the LGBT community.

We cannot continue to have organizations, movements or programs that exclude large portions of our community, and yet call ourselves "conscious." This is both hypocritical and contradictory. The majority of our population is composed of women. They must be empowered just like men. A growing number of our community members are gay, lesbian, bisexual, etc. As Black people, they need protection and empowerment too.

Further dividing an already fragmented Black community only serves the agenda of our enemies (who lest we forget, seek to exploit and control Black people regardless of our gender or sexuality). Furthermore, we need to realize that **all types** of Black people, including feminists and members of the LGBT community, participated in the Black liberation struggle. Who are we to now exclude them from our love and service? This does not mean we need to march in gay parades, join a Black feminist organization, or embrace lifestyles or ideologies we disagree with. It does mean that we should not ban these communities from our organizations, insult them, or act as if they are not members of our family and nation.

The Limitations of Boycotting as a Protest Tactic

The repeated occurrence of police brutality and the killing of innocent Black people is unacceptable. These tragedies continue to inspire national outrage among black people. It also inspired activists and others to **do something** about this injustice.

One of the most prominent ideas that emerged from the tragic killing of Mike Brown in Ferguson, Missouri was the national call for black people to boycott white retail establishments on "Black Friday," "Cyber Monday," and in some cases, indefinitely.

We heard a similar call when George Zimmerman was cleared of criminal charges for murdering innocent teen Trayvon Martin in Florida. The resistance/protest strategy in that case was for black people to launch a national boycott against the state of Florida, with a focus on its tourism and retail industries. The battle cry was, "*Don't shop in Florida, don't buy products from Florida, and don't vacation in Florida!"*

As a rule, organizing strategies and tactics should be relevant to the issue at hand and strategically designed to produce desired outcomes. The tragic killing of Michael Brown in Ferguson, Missouri demonstrates unbridled police brutality and documents how the state murders Black people without remorse or consequence.

The simple question for us then, is "How does boycotting retail businesses eliminate or reduce the assault or murder of black people by hyper violent and over-militarized police?

I am all for boycotting malicious and greedy corporations in an effort to use our $1.1 trillion purchasing power with people and in ways that empower us. Nevertheless, this tactic does not adequately address and resolve the issue of police brutality.

Effective boycotts target institutions or businesses directly responsible for the oppression we are challenging, or closely involved/invested in entities that **are** directly responsible.

For example, the 1955-56 Montgomery bus boycott that catapulted Martin Luther King to national recognition, made sense. Black people in Montgomery were tired of paying the same bus fare as whites, but having no power to choose where they sat on the bus. Furthermore, we paid our fare on the front of the bus, and then had to get off and board via the back doors. White bus drivers often took off without allowing black people who already paid to board the bus!

The injustice did not stop there. Once on the bus, we had to sit in the "colored section." In addition, if the white seating section became overcrowded, we had to relinquish our seats to white passengers! Rosa Parks was arrested if you recall, for refusing to relinquish her seat.

Activists in Montgomery, primarily Black women, made a good call by asking Black folk not to ride public buses. Why should we support a company or service that cheats and mistreats us? The rest, as you know, was history.

In this case white retail stores - while guilty of harassing Black shoppers, charging exorbitant prices, and underpaying Black workers - do not murder us and are not directly tied to the police that do.

If we choose to boycott, it should target either the police or court institutions or institutions directly involved with or supportive of them. Courts and law enforcement agencies do not sell retail items to the public. Therefore, we cannot boycott them, and we have yet to identify outside institutions that directly support their ability to attack and kill us. A boycott simply is not relevant or effective given these considerations.

There is another major point for us to consider. By targeting establishments not responsible for police brutality, we potentially punish "innocent" people or institutions (innocent of committing police brutality, at least).

Since many black people work as cashiers, sales clerks, and low-level managers in U.S. retail establishments, the boycott being called for will likely cause many black folk to lose much-needed jobs in a **very tough** economy. How do we justify a tactic that punishes innocent people and negatively affects US, more than it does our opposition?

For these reasons, I do not believe a nationwide boycott of U.S. retail stores will effectively address or resolve the issue of anti-Black police brutality,

There are, to be fair, some advantages to boycotting: doing so will keep the issue alive in public discourse, create and promote Black solidarity, and raise consciousness among our people while mobilizing us to resist our oppression.

However, as already mentioned, the targets of the boycott are too broad and vaguely defined, they are not necessarily responsible for the issue we raise, nor do these businesses wield the power or responsibility to resolve the problem. In addition, the boycott can result in massive layoffs that may harm us more than it punishes our opponents.

Nevertheless, the idea of boycotting has many supporters, is gaining ground, and has a few advantages like those identified above. To be clear, I support Black resistance to oppression, and I applaud and generally support attempts to make us active agents of our own solidarity and liberation. To be clear, I am not suggesting that we abandon the tactic of boycotting businesses. I am suggesting that we tweak this tactics and use it selectively to make it more relevant and effective.

In conclusion and going forward, perhaps we can target a **specific** retail chain or other institution that is highly supportive of police, donates money to murderous police officers or "Police Benevolent Associations," or that has publicly defended their acts of aggression against us. Even this would not definitively end or reduce police brutality, but it would at least target those responsible – those who collaborate with or defend belligerent police, and actual police guilty of assaulting and killing Black people with impunity.

Lastly, it might also be a good idea to couple a "Buy Black" movement with a boycott. We can develop a list of Black-owned businesses throughout the U.S. that provide important goods/services we desire, and help Black businesses and Black consumers simultaneously. Of course, these businesses would show their appreciation by lowering prices in return for their increased sales volume.

But even these boycott tweaks will prove to be of minimal influence if we fail to openly and persistently confront, embarrass, disrupt and neutralize police precincts, prosecutors' offices, courthouses, and propagandist news networks (like Fox) that defend police, devalue Black life, and mischaracterize activists fighting for justice and peace in this nation. Black Consciousness, Black Power!

How to Identify Compromised or Fraudulent Black Leaders

A world dominated by violence, deception, and injustice becomes a breeding ground for leaders, pundits (social commentators) and activists/organizers. These individuals take many forms including formal organization leaders, politicians, bloggers, public speakers, journalists, TV personalities, nonprofit organizers, grassroots activists, etc.

It is inspiring to know that some people are courageous enough to challenge oppressive systems, inform us and even organize us to improve our quality of life. Unfortunately, not all of these people are genuine. Some are thoroughly hedonist and motivated by the all-too-familiar goals of fame, wealth, comfort and status. Of course, being self-absorbed does not mean a person is incompetent. Many of these individuals are intelligent and skilled. They simply care more about themselves than they do the people they supposedly lead. They may have grand dreams of driving expensive cars, purchasing fine homes, exerting authority over people, or having their pick of sexual activity with throngs of admiring and gullible followers.

We all desire some degree of material comfort and we all want the respect and admiration of others. Dr. Martin Luther King discussed this in a sermon entitled **"The Drum Major Instinct."** Drawing from Biblical references, Dr. King reminds us that the desire for recognition, importance, leadership and "greatness" sometimes leads us to focus on satisfying our appetites for such things, rather than doing what really makes us great: *serving others*.

We find this drum major instinct among some leaders in the Black community. For these individuals, the goal of empowering Black people is really a noble-sounding disguise for empowering themselves at Black people's expense. Some begin their careers with good intentions, but like the character Anakin Skywalker in the movie *"Star Wars,"* become compromised and corrupted by their arrogance, fear or an obsessive need for personal power and authority.

This phenomenon does not just occur in science fiction movies. Back in 2014, the New York Daily News broke a story that implicated longtime activist Al Sharpton as a FBI informant.[34] Allegedly, Sharpton attempted to gain information on the whereabouts of Assata

---

[34] http://www.nydailynews.com/new-york/activist-recalls-1983-meeting-sharpton-bugged-briefcase-article-1.1754857

Shakur, who was on the run from law enforcement after escaping from prison in 1979. According to the Smoking Gun website, Sharpton also wore a wire to gain incriminating information on mob bosses for the government.

Once exposed to the benefits of fame, wealth, travel sexual favors, etc., some lose their way. What began as a sincere effort to help uplift the Black community morphs into a desire to satisfy their personal appetites. The desire to serve the community dwindles and the desire for applause, power, comfort and recognition become supreme. Instead of valuing constructive criticism, these folk resent what they falsely view as jealous challenges to their leadership or authority. Compromised Black people/leaders begin to demonstrate some or all of the following behaviors:

- They attempt to silence or attack critics

- They develop feelings of entitlement and elitism

- Seeking shortcuts or alternatives to years of solid study, work, and activism, compromised leaders resort to get-rich-quick schemes, poorly planned projects, and in the worst cases, fraudulent activities or dishonesty about their credentials or past achievements.

- They create cult-like organizations to satisfy their appetites for sex, money, recognition and unchecked power and influence.

- They are reluctant to collaborate with others or seek outside expertise and opinion; their inflated egos compel them to lead or micromanage everything, even programs or movements for which they are *unqualified*.

- Because of their obsessive desire for money and power, they are easily seduced to become paid government agents/informants.

- They take high-paying jobs, occupy important positions or associate with people/organizations that oppress their people and compromise their leadership.

Such behavior leads the larger Black community to great disillusionment, failure and deception. We have the right and responsibility to protect ourselves against such fraudulent and compromised individuals. Fortunately, there are things we can do to protect ourselves. These things take the form of questions or things to look for:

Are they qualified? Simply put, you want to know if someone is qualified to do the work they proclaim to do, either through education, life experience or both. In addition, if the person blatantly lies about their qualifications, be wary of them. People who truly care about community empowerment will do the work/study necessary to provide excellent service.

Do they display humility and gratitude? Authentic leaders do not attempt to take all the credit for community victories, refer to themselves as the reincarnation of a great leader from the past, or repeatedly brag about their accomplishments. **Other people** speak about them with admiration and respect or recall their accomplishments. Authentic leaders should thank the community and individuals for their support. Here is an interesting bit of advice. Pay attention to a person's use of pronouns. Do they always use the words "me" and I"?" On the other hand, do you hear them often say "We," "us," and "our?" This often provides clues to whether a person is self-absorbed or whether they focus on the collective. As no one is perfect and we all make errors in judgment or fall short, you also want to know if this person is accountable. Do they apologize when they fall short, or do they blame others and attempt to shift responsibility away from themselves? Do they admit when they do not know something, or do they avoid and attempt to refocus the question?

You want signs that the person has successfully collaborated with others in the past. No leader can be effective without working with others. This means there should be evidence of teamwork and collaboration in a person's background. If a person does everything him or herself, this is a sign of trouble.

The person should have a documented background of successful leadership and activism: This separates genuine leaders from "talking heads" and mere social commentators. What organization did they lead or belong to? What role did they play in the organization? Did they bring honor and success to the organization, or shame and failure? This research should reveal a general record of jobs well-done, effective organizing, and good reports from those the person worked with in the community. Compromised leaders will often display evidence of stealing, poor decision-making, dishonesty, self-absorption or other negative behaviors in their past experiences. Good or bad leaders are not born overnight.

Who are their mentors? Effective leaders are typically guided and advised by wise and credible mentors. The politics, reputation, and past activities of mentors also reveal things to us about those they advise. Compromised leaders will often have no mentors or have very questionable ones with shaky backgrounds/beliefs themselves. In addition, mentors who are credible can and will vouch for those they mentored. If a person's mentors are unwilling to vouch for them, or if they speak negatively about them, this naturally raises suspicions.

What do the people who live in the community where this person organized in the past have to say about them? If someone did organizing in a particular city, people in that community should have favorable memories of this person and their work.

Do they have a plan, program or platform designed to improve conditions in our community? Anyone can give an opinion or complain about injustice. Leaders distinguish themselves by providing relevant analysis, methods, strategies, and plans to **address important issues and solve problems**. In addition, you should see evidence of this person implementing these methods or solutions.

Do they just proclaim and pontificate, or do they educate and inform? Genuine leaders work hard to teach and inform the masses to do better and be better. They expose societal and in-house contradictions, teach people how oppressive systems work, and equip people with the knowledge or tools to challenge injustice and discard self-defeating thoughts and behavior. To do this of course, the leader must have this knowledge or skill set themselves.

Do they see themselves as THE leader of Black people, or one of many? The limits of the messiah complex are self-explanatory and well known. But here is another point to consider: *Genuine leaders work to develop and produce other people to assume leadership,* because they realize no one person (regardless of their talent or intelligence) can truly empower or liberate millions of Black people!

If you ask yourself these questions and do the proper research, you will most likely be able to distinguish genuine and effective leaders from those who are compromised, incompetent, or fraudulent. Doing this will protect you from wasting time, money and loyalty to those who do not deserve such things. Taking this approach does not make you an enemy of the people, but a wise and informed person.

Finally, do not assume that wide popularity, a full schedule of speaking engagements, or recognition in social or traditional media makes a person authentic or effective as a leader or activist. Sometimes these are indicators of legitimate accomplishment. Sometimes, this just means someone has an effective publicist and marketing strategy. It could also mean that the people supporting this person are uninformed and gullible sheeple that drank the propaganda Kool-Aid! As powerful Hip Hop artist Immortal Technique says in his song, "Industrial Revolution, *"Cause if you go platinum, it's got nothing to do with luck, it just means that a million people are stupid as fuck."*

Measuring the Effectiveness of Our Organizations

Creating or joining a Black organization is one thing. Leading one is another; Leading one effectively is another matter altogether. An important part of the process involves evaluation. By this, I refer to an accurate way of determining if we are leading *effectively*. Without a reliable evaluation method, we have no way of determining if our organizations are successful.

This article will attempt to create a very basic form of leadership evaluation using questions in various themes. A more thorough method might involve scoring each section and would establish a range of scores representing poor, average, good and exceptional designations (this method is, as I explained, *basic and leaves room for elaboration and expansion*). However, I do believe this battery of questions can help us evaluate and improve our organizations.

VISION/MISSION: A measurement of how successful we are in communicating our organizational purpose and objectives

1. Do we have a clear vision of our purpose and the people we serve?

2. Do we have a clear sense of how we fulfill our purpose?

3. Are both of these clearly worded, written and distributed/taught to our members?

4. Do our members demonstrate an accurate knowledge of the vision and mission?

INTEGRITY: A measurement of the extent to which what our organization does aligns with its stated objectives/values.

1. Do our group meetings, programs/events, decisions, expenditures, and issues we raise/address coincide with, reinforce and advocate our stated vision, purpose, and the people we serve?

2. What is our membership's opinion on the previous question?

3. Are leaders taught to make organizational decisions based on the organization's vision and mission?

TRAINING: A measurement of how successful we are in building leadership capacity within our organization.

1. Does our group have a formal process for identifying and grooming/mentoring new leadership and building leadership capacity?

2. Does this process work? Do the people we train demonstrate they have the skills, habits and knowledge needed to effectively lead the group?

3. Do we provide hands-on opportunities for such people to grow into effective leaders?

4. Is our training both theoretical and practical (hands-on)?

5. Do we delegate responsibility in ways that develop important leadership skills and experience?

ARCHIVES: Measuring how effective we are in recording, storing, and using our organization's history.

1. Does our organization have a historian or archivist responsible for recording and storing events and documents?

2. Do we have a way of determining what material is relevant to record and keep?

3. Do we make audiovisual recordings of our programs, speakers and events?

4. Do we use various means of storing important recordings, documents, and photographs (physical file cabinets, online storage)?

5. Does our membership have access to our historical documents?

6. Do we have a system of encrypting and backing up our files?

7. Are the files and materials we record stored safely? Do we take precautions to insure that our materials are protected from fire/water damage or oxidation?

8. Do we actually use these files in our meetings or leadership training?

9. Are the files/materials well-organized and easy to search and find?

OUTREACH: A measurement of how well our organization communicates with other organizations and people in the larger community

1. Do people in our community know we exist? Are they familiar with the services we provide? Have we identified popular places in the community where our people congregate, and do we distribute our literature and promotional materials to these places?

2. Are the fliers, articles, advertisements, social media posts, etc. we create to announce our events distributed or posted at least two weeks prior to the event?

3. Do we set and achieve specific goals for attendance at our meetings and events?

4. Have we established criteria for determining what makes an event "well" or poorly attended?

Agyei Tyehimba, My Two Cents

5. Do the same people attend our meetings or events, or do we notice a significant number of new faces?

6. Do we rely only on the officers of our organization to do outreach, or do we involve lay members in this process as well?

7. Do we conduct outreach in our larger community to develop relationships with like-minded groups the people we serve?

GENERAL BODY MEETINGS

1. Are organizational meetings reliable and consistent (Do they occur in the same place, time and location, or do these variables change often?)

2. Do our meetings start and end promptly?

3. Are the meetings we convene fun, informative and inspiring?

4. Do we disseminate or post written agendas for each meeting to our members? Do we follow the agenda, or do our meetings often steer off into unrelated matters?

5. Are general body members (those who are not in leadership positions) given time to voice their opinions or ideas?

6. Do we always have a secretary present to record minutes of our meetings?

7. Are meeting minutes posted online, in our office and/or in a newsletter to reach members that miss meetings?

8. Do we use our meetings to resolve issues, raise issues, debate ideas, and solicit assistance?

9. If we decide on doing something as an organization, do we set a specific timetable for when tasks should be completed? Do we determine specific people responsible for completing tasks?

10. Can members critique decisions or actions of the organization openly and without being ostracized?

11. Are criticisms or ideas from members actually considered and/or implemented by the leadership?

12. Do leaders debrief/review after general body meetings?

CHARACTER/PERSONAL INTEGRITY

1. Do organization leaders do what they say, when they say they will?

2. Do leaders submit paperwork or complete important tasks in a timely manner?

3. When leaders communicate with outside people, do they promptly follow-up with those people via phone or email?

4. Are leaders accessible to general body members (office hours, phone, email, and social media)?

5. Do leaders respond to phone calls or emails from members or others within one to two business days?

PROGRAMMING

1. Does our organization do events that inform and inspire members?

2. Does our programming reflect the vision and mission of our organization?

3. Do our events duplicate those of other organizations or do they unique and creative?

4. Do we use our events to promote our organization, recruit new members and solicit assistance?

5. Do our events draw good attendance?

6. Does our programming meet the needs of our membership?

7. Do we use our resources (financial and otherwise) to protect and advocate for the vulnerable and voiceless members of our larger community?

8. Do we have a system for asking members what programming they would like our organization to sponsor? Do we actively involve members to help coordinate, promote and participate in our events?

MORALE: A measurement of how well we inspire pride and positive feelings about our organization from our members.

1. Does our organization do a good job of promoting the benefits of joining our group?

2. Do we use promotional materials to instill a sense of pride and belonging (t-shirts, buttons, bumper stickers)?

3. Does the leadership officially recognize and publicly celebrate the achievements and contributions of individual members?

4. Do we create events that provide opportunities for our members to meet, encourage, and fellowship with each other?

These are just a few categories we need to consider in evaluating our organizations. I hope that you find this information helpful. Our organizations must strive for excellence and effectiveness because so many people depend on them.

Part III

"Stand Up!"

(Confronting our external oppressors and building programs, institutions and movements to empower and liberate ourselves)

A Black Power Outline (My Manifesto)

You will notice this article is entitled "A" not "THE" Black Power Outline. This is to connote that it is not the definitive, exclusive, or "divine" plan - just my own thoughts on how to transform our collective condition in the United States. The reference to an outline, suggests that this is not an exhaustive plan. Everything is not spelled out or filled in here, nor should it be. Use your imagination and intelligence and apply or reject as you see fit.

Finally, this plan is not novel, new, or any indication of some "genius" on my part, but simply an attempt to apply some common sense and draw from great minds of the past. You will also notice that the following remarks draw from a number of my previous articles that generally address the questions of how we are oppressed, why we are oppressed, and what we must do to liberate and empower ourselves.

What I Believe:

I believe that our people (though imperfect like others) are beautiful and valuable. We have the rights to "Life, liberty, and the pursuit of happiness, with or without man or a document's validation or recognition of such rights. This oft-quoted phrase implies a number of issues (healthcare, incarceration, employment, etc.) We have an obligation to do everything in our power to continue the fight of our ancestors and ensure these things for ourselves and our children.

I believe that we cannot allow any religion, philosophy or idea to blind us to fundamental truths we know and observe. I believe any faith or philosophy we subscribe to should either advance us in the previously mentioned ways, we should modify them to do so, or abandon them in favor of those that do.

I believe it is our primary responsibility to solve our problems, and that we have the right to select the methods, people or resources to do so. I believe our enemies are white supremacy, corporate greed and corruption, and government repression as manifested through imperialism, forced poverty, war, hunger, mass incarceration, urban decline, socially engineered fear, etc.

I believe many agents of these social ills exist of various forms. Therefore, in a larger sense, our "enemies" are those that support, promote or defend injustice, avarice, and oppression regardless of race, gender, or other designations. Finally, I firmly believe that even if we didn't read another book, view another documentary, listen to another speech, take another class or attend another conference, we have enough accumulated knowledge, experience and skills to do something **right now** to empower and liberate ourselves.

If you find all of this to be nonsense, please accept my apologies in advance. If you find the following ideas helpful or even partially valid, then teach ***and apply them.*** The true credit in my opinion goes to Marcus Garvey, Elijah Muhammad, and Malcolm X- three of our greatest Black Power theorists in my opinion. You will find that many modern-day expressions of Black Nationalism draw heavily from their ideas.

Now that my disclaimers and introductions are done, let us journey together in thought to explore the thinking and actions required for our freedom and empowerment. In a society that uses enormous resources to keep Black people confused, bitter, disorganized and powerless, any discussion of how to reverse such conditions is extremely important and radical. Therefore, I hope you will continue reading and apply what you find useful.

On August 3, 1857, Frederick Douglass delivered his "West Indian Emancipation" speech. Most people only quote two paragraphs of his speech, because they speak so well to the nature of resistance. The truth of Frederick Douglass' famous words concerning power and resistance continue to resonate with truth and relevance, and we should keep these words present in our minds:

Let me give you a word of the philosophy of reform. The whole history of the progress of human liberty shows that all concessions yet made to her august claims have been born of earnest struggle.

The conflict has been exciting, agitating, all-absorbing, and for the time being, putting all other tumults to silence. It must do this or it does nothing. If there is no struggle there is no progress. Those who profess to favor freedom and yet deprecate agitation are men who want crops without plowing up the ground; they want rain without thunder and lightning. They want the ocean without the awful roar of its many waters.

This struggle may be a moral one, or it may be a physical one, and it may be both moral and physical, but it must be a struggle. Power concedes nothing without a demand. It never did and it never will. Find out just what any people will quietly submit to and you have found out the exact measure of injustice and wrong which will be imposed upon them, and these will continue till they are resisted with either words or blows, or with both. The limits of tyrants are prescribed by the endurance of those whom they oppress.

In this spirit, allow me to suggest the following:

1. In an era where everyone speaks of "humanity," Black people still are more impoverished, incarcerated, stigmatized, and disproportionately victimized than most other people (despite actual and perceived "progress"). Blacks fight for "humanity," while other members of the human family fail to reciprocate. Given this reality, we need people who advocate for Black advancement without apology or explanation to anyone else. In the old days, such people were referred to as "race" men or women.

2. We all have adopted various religious and political philosophies that sometimes are at odds. However, regardless of this, Black

Christians, Buddhists, Muslims, Jews, atheists, those who practice indigenous African religions, capitalists, Marxists, nationalists, etc. at any given moment face police brutality, failing schools, health issues, poverty and racism. It is easy to say the oft-repeated slogan, "We must learn to work together to resolve our problems and uplift our people." However, this implies that we understand and implement a strategy Brother Malcolm suggested and what Dr. Maulana Karenga terms "Operational Unity." This means that we organize around ideals/issues that a majority of us value and agree upon, then create institutions, movements, and projects where we actually work together despite our differences to create change and empower ourselves. Chancellor Williams in his classic book, "The Destruction of Black Civilization," warned us about the dangers of continued disunity:

> *Just as it is in the case of africa and black people everywhere, the central problem of over 30 million blacks in america is unity...the picture of several thousand black organizations, each independent and vying for leadership, is substantially the same picture of fragmentation and disunity in africa that led to the downfall of the entire race. We have often seen that even in earlier times very often all that was involved was that somebody wanted to be the "head," was not getting there fast enough, and therefore, organized his own little state. Most of them perished, picked off one by one. The same thing will happen to any black organizations, standing alone, that disturb the white mind."*

3. We have lost a great majority of our youth who have been seduced to ignorance, violence, apathy, indifference and materialism because we have failed to properly guide them. We cannot depend on public schools as they currently exist to properly prepare our children

to become leaders and problem-solvers for our people. These schools prepare our children to be obedient low-wage workers for other people or cheap labor in American penal institutions. We must organize leadership training programs, community centers, homeschooling programs, independent African-centered schools, Saturday schools, and Rites of Passage programs to rescue and reclaim our youth.

4. Black working class communities are under serious attack. Gentrification has diluted our political and cultural power in communities around the country with an influx of entitled whites and Bourgeois Blacks who rob such places of their cultural and political integrity. We must begin an aggressive program to purchase property, develop and maintain our cultural institutions, and create financial institutions like community credit unions. Such institutions provide the money so necessary to start community cooperatives/businesses, provide employment and redevelop our communities.

5. Wealthy and socially conscious Black entertainers, athletes and professionals must be organized, politicized, and called upon to invest some of their wealth and networks to help build quality Black schools, realty companies, supermarkets, lobbying groups, hospitals and other institutions/programs so vital to true community development.

6. Black people continue to face unbridled brutality at the hands of racist/fascist police, white citizens, and predatory Black people. Like **Robert F. Williams** and Malcolm X, I support the right of our people to protect ourselves and our families from such victimization. Every time a cop for example, kills one of us, is exonerated, and keeps his/her job, it sends the general public a message that we are

not valuable and that we are "easy and unprotected prey." Prayer, candlelight vigils, tearful funeral testimonials and marches have not made a *dent* in this issue.

Therefore, we must create the capacity to defend and protect our communities from those who prey upon them, while pursuing older and more traditional methods. It is shameful that we neglect to do this out of fear or cowardly interpretations of scripture. If gang members can intimidate and terrorize Black communities, if Black military officers can fight and kill for American interests all over the world, perhaps someone should organize and politicize them to use that same energy to protect our own men, women, children and elders. Contrary to popular opinion, our lives are just as valuable as anyone else's life

7. Our identity and citizenship extend beyond local, state and national boundaries created by men. We are an African people (although largely disconnected) whether we admit it or not. In the Pan African tradition of Garvey and Malcolm, we must establish business and political relationships with black and brown people in Africa and throughout the world.

This relationship should not be self-serving or simply around commercial interests. As members of the African Diaspora, we should actively expose and protest imperialism and corporate exploitation throughout the world. An international presence and network will prove mutually beneficial toward this end and in several other ways.

When establishing such global relationships, we should avoid the mistake of adopting America's "enemies" or "allies" as our own. The enslaved should not share the logic of the enslaver because both have opposing interests and values. Dr. Maulana Karenga refers to this concept as "oppositional logic." The time has come for us to accurate understand who the true "terrorists" and champions of freedom truly are, from our own vantage points.

The late Nelson Mandela demonstrated the principle of oppositional logic powerfully during his visit to the United States following his release from prison in 1990. A white man in the New York City College audience criticized Mandela for praising Fidel Castro, Muammar Gadaffi, Yasser Arafat, and other International leaders who the United States defined as "terrorists." Without missing a beat, the venerable human rights leader and South African revolutionary responded,

> *One of the mistakes that some political analysts make is to think that their enemies should be our enemies. That, we can and will never do. We have our own struggle...we are grateful to the world for supporting our struggle. But nevertheless, we are an independent organization with its own policies...Yasser Arafat, Colonel Gadaffi, Fidel Castro support our struggle to the hilt. Our attitude is based solely on the fact that they fully support the anti-apartheid struggle. They do not support it only in rhetoric. They put are placing resources at our disposal for us to wage our struggle...*[35]

---

[35] 1990 Town Hall Meeting with Nelson Mandela In NYC. You can view at: https://www.youtube.com/watch?v=q6eE9BlUfBg

8. We must understand how politics really works (See "A Word About Politics and Voting"), and understand how we've historically made progress in America. Politics has less to do with morality or ethics, and more to do with power, leverage and organized pressure. National elections are a complete sham, and do not produce benefits commensurate with the time, money and energy we invest in them. We should definitely control local politics in territories with a Black majority and/or sizeable population, and we should seriously study the deceased Mayor Chokwe Lumumba's plan for Jackson, Mississippi, which was developed by the Malcolm X Grassroots Movement.[36] In places where we are not in the majority, we must amass and wield wealth and power to pressure those in power to do our bidding. How? By being in a position to tangibly support or pose a threat to their image, comfort, safety, plans, or finances and by disrupting their ability to operate normally. Check history and see if I am misleading you on this matter.

9. Notwithstanding religious doctrine, comic books, sci-fi thrillers, or cults, no one man or woman is coming to save Black people or has the power to do so. We can go farther and suggest that no one man or woman has ever done so. Black empowerment and liberation requires a collective effort. This means we must practice and encourage "All hands on deck" organizing (Black solidarity). We must work with serious-minded organizations and individuals in our community, even as we challenge and critique policies and methods with which we

---

[36] You can view this plan here: https://mxgm.org/the-jackson-plan-a-struggle-for-self-determination-participatory-democracy-and-economic-justice/

disagree. Not all Black people will ever reach complete agreement on anything, and we should not expect this. Not all white folk agree, nor do all of them belong to any one organization. They experience in-fighting and bitter rivalries as we do. However, they do agree on one thing: that they will maintain power, wealth, and control over others....

10. Related to the previous point is the realization that *no one* regardless of how long they've served us, how well they've served us, their wealth, amount of wisdom, speaking ability, past achievements, number of followers, political title, etc. is beyond constructive and valid criticism. We are human after all, and therefore prone to dishonesty, opportunism, ego and errors in judgment. We must not only welcome constructive criticism and principled debate among each other, we must embrace it.

11. Many of us (hopefully) know that the 13th Amendment to the Constitution created a new form of enslavement called incarceration. The American incarceration rate grew an incredible 700% between 1970-2005, largely because of the nefarious "War on drugs."[37] 60% of America's prison population is composed of Black and Latino people. 1 in 3 Black men will be in prison in their lifetime. Then there is the issue of Black political prisoners, many of whom languish in American dungeons due to their political beliefs, not criminal activity. Once imprisoned, inmates are forced to work for as little as 25 cents

---

[37] The Huffington Post has an excellent article on the subject of incarceration and the war on drugs: http://www.huffingtonpost.com/2013/04/08/drug-war-mass-incarceration_n_3034310.html

to $1 an hour. In addition, they do not just make license plates or repair furniture. Today's inmates make just about every product you can think of including: headphones, home appliances, office furniture, airplane parts, military and medical supplies and food products.[38] Many prisons are now privatized. Shareholders earn enormous profits from prison labor without the hassle of strikes, paying unemployment benefits or providing vacation time. The prison industry is indeed a new form of enslavement or cheap and non-unionized pool of Black labor and therefore we are compelled to address this major civil, human rights, and labor issue with a serious movement for prison reform. In the meantime, we must spend significant resources and energy to help our people in captivity secure the educational, mental health, and other rehabilitative and transitional services they need upon their release.[39] When one of us is chained, none of us are free.

12. All multi-national corporations believe in a god and its name is profit. Their tenacious drive for expansion and profit has led to genetically engineered food products, electoral corruption, war mongering, environmental pollution, mass unemployment, and the repression of dissent among other things. The people must wage a movement to dismantle or at minimum severely regulate these

---

[38] http://atlantablackstar.com/2014/10/10/12-mainstream-corporations-benefiting-from-the-prison-industrial-complex/

[39] Soffiyah Elijah, a longtime prisoner rights activist, attorney for political prisoners, and legal scholar on the issue of prison reform, does excellent work for incarcerated brothers and sisters through the Correctional Association of NY.

bloodsuckers. In very real ways, they are possibly the greatest threat to global peace, justice, environmental vitality and health.

13. The fight for freedom, justice and equality must be **total**. No man, woman or child should be victimized by discrimination, brutality or deprivation. In the truly liberated society, racism, imperialism, class exploitation, patriarchy, or sexuality-based oppression will not exist, or at minimum, will exist with maximum accountability and consequences. Dr. Joy Degruy's concept of Post Traumatic Slave Syndrome is real! Much of our self-hatred, tendency toward violence with each other, family molestation, domestic violence, ego and jealousy stem from over 400 years of mistreatment and propaganda.[40] Hurt people, hurt people. Therefore, we must create organizations and programs to address the mental health issues that plague our community.

14. We must teach our people to value study and research aimed to solve our problems. Knowledge is not something we acquire to win money on a television game show or feel important at the expense of our brothers or sisters. We must revitalize and/or create Black think tanks composed of activists and intellectuals who focus on researching our and others' past liberation movements, leaders, in addition to the blueprints and critical ideas/programs they produced. Times and the tools that accompany them, have changed in some cases, but there is no need to "reinvent the wheel." Some of our dedicated and effective

---

[40] Leary, Joy DeGruy. Post Traumatic Slave Syndrome : America's Legacy of Enduring Injury and Healing. Milwaukie, Oregon :Uptone Press, 2005. Print.

people and organizations of the past have already done important work and posed effective solutions that many of us today have not seriously studied, reviewed, and tried to implement! To maintain focus and integrity, these think tanks cannot accept even one penny from outside corporations, government agencies or universities. These think tanks will constantly share their findings with community leaders and organizations and make themselves available for presentations/consultation to help these leaders and organizations solve the problems they face, based on strategic thinking and sound analysis.

Resolving the Problem of Black Miseducation

We are familiar with the oft-quoted Ghanaian proverb, "It takes a village to raise a child." Sometimes I wonder if we recognize that "It takes a village to destroy a child" as well.

With this in mind, we cannot attach sole responsibility for the miseducation of our youth to negligent Black households. While easy and convenient, this approach fails to assign equal responsibility to our local places of worship, community organizations, and public schools.

Of these, the last community resource (public schools) remains convenient targets for those of us working to provide Black children with an empowering education. But if it takes a village, why do we single public schools out when it comes to education? For one, they are THE recognized institution responsible for education in our communities; Secondly, they have trained teachers, administrators and staff (whose salaries derive from our taxes); In addition, schools have budgets, supplies, and property, specifically allocated and designated for educating our children. Certainly, this all makes sense, that is until we recognize that the public education system has a hidden agenda for educating Black children that draws its roots from the turn of the 20th century.

This hidden agenda implies that we must begin by clearly understanding the purpose and objectives of education from a societal view. Richard Schaull, writing in the 30th anniversary edition of Paolo Friere's classic text, *Pedagogy of the Oppressed*, summarizes Friere's position on the purpose of education beautifully:

There is no such thing as neutral education. Education either functions as an instrument which is used to facilitate integration of the younger generation into the logic of the present system and bring about conformity or it becomes the practice of freedom, the means by which men and women deal critically and creatively with reality and discover how to participate in the transformation of their world.

Putting this quote into context, the U.S. educational system prepares our children to integrate and conform to its culture of values, expectations and laws. From the societal standpoint, our children are educated to assume three primary roles: 1.To become a semi-skilled and obedient pool of labor (for corporations). 2. To become a relatively smaller pool of directors or managers (professional overseers) for the corporate plantation. 3. To become the defenders and enforcers (military and police) of the corporate culture.

The first group is designed to generate wealth via their underpaid labor for the corporate elite while the second group coordinates, manages and helps train the first group or uses its higher degree of skill to make more money for the corporate culture. The third group monitors, detains, intimidates and murders critics, rebels and disillusioned citizens who might threaten the corporate culture's existence and objectives. You will note that all groups must be patriotic, subscribe to bourgeois notions of achieving the "American Dream," defend and sympathize with U.S. capitalist/imperialist culture, and of course have the basic skills and sensibilities to fulfill their respective functions.

Black Nationalists like me and my comrades in the educational trenches, find the social conditioning and conformity agenda of education unjust and unacceptable. We side with the freedom-oriented and transformative objectives of education. We reject an educational system that produces generations of people who uphold, defend and cooperate with an unjust and hegmonic status quo. We seek one that creates critical and creative thinkers and problem-solvers who work to create a just society. We want competent and compassionate human beings who identify with and advocate for the Black experiences and communities that birthed them. Knowing that the traditional school system - along with the university think tanks, foundations, and corporate culture that created and maintained it - aims to create people who will maintain the current status quo, we challenge and reject it. We understand that such curricula, schools, and school cultures will keep the current system of white supremacy in place. *Our unashamed goal is to dismantle it and prevent it from regenerating.*

For many of us then, African-centered schools become the remedy of choice. By definition, such schools boast all-Black faculty and staff, use fair and effective methods of discipline that edify rather than humiliate, and promote academic rigor and competence while teaching our children to love, understand, advance and protect their history, minds, and people. Dr. Mwalimu Shujaa, a widely recognized expert on the subject, outlined five characteristics/objectives of African-centered education in his book, *Too Much Schooling, Too Little Education:*

1. It should reflect our own interests as a cultural nation and be grounded in our cultural history.

2. It should be a process of healthy identity development.

3. It should provide for the inter-generational transmission of values, beliefs, traditions, customs, rituals and sensibilities along with the knowledge of why these things must be sustained.

4. It should teach children how to determine what is in our interests, distinguish our interests from those of others, and recognize when our interests are consistent and inconsistent with those of others.

5. It should prepare children to accept the staff of cultural leadership from the generation that preceded theirs, build upon their inheritance, and make ready the generation that will follow them

Likewise, Dr. Molefi Asante, regarded as a leading scholar of Afrocentrism notes that an African-centered education should:

(1) Foster the development of "proper" relationships between the student and their family, community and creator (2) Generate solutions for issues and concerns facing Africa and African people throughout the Diaspora and (3) Develop moral social leadership skills in each student.

Before we all lock arms, close our eyes and begin singing "Kumbaya" however, we must acknowledge some serious challenges to resolving the issue of Black miseducation. No serious movement to provide our children a real education will occur easily or without opposition, as it challenges the aims of the United States empire itself. Therefore, we must consider the following:

Because true African-centered curricula and schools go against the social conditioning agenda of the U.S. empire, they face intense scrutiny, monitoring, and lack of support from "mainstream" society who will label them as "reverse racist," "separatist," and even "terrorist." Such schools therefore, will need to seek private funding and avoid any government support. They will most likely need to be private and independent, and charge tuition to cover expenses.

There are not enough Afrocentric schools to accommodate all or even 10% of the school-aged Black children and youth in the United States: According to the National Center for Education Statistics, in 2014, approximately 7.7 million Black children attended public elementary and secondary schools. From my internet search, I could only barely identify 37 African-centered schools in the **entire**

country and I could not verify that all of them are still open, or are in fact, truly African-centered. It will likely take decades to close this gap. In the meantime, *this means the overwhelming majority of our children will attend traditional public schools*. Certainly, we should begin a rigorous campaign to create viable independent and African-centered schools.

However, at the same time, we need dedicated and qualified Black teachers to continue working in *existing* public schools, providing our children with a conscious alternative to the brainwashing and social conditioning they will likely receive in those institutions. We also need to create more viable after school programs and liberation schools in our community centers and places of worship. Our churches, mosques and temples own property and have already-established congregations/members, many of whom have expertise in several important fields in additional to professional resources. Congregants should challenge these institutions to create such programs.

Another excellent option is community homeschooling. Brother Markus Kline in Chicago has created three successful home schools called Freedom Home Academy. Each accommodates more than 20 students, and provides a rigorous academic and African-centered education. Students learn three languages (Arabic, Swahili, and French) and ADVANCED academics. All students demonstrate accelerated learning. Why can't we create schools like this in every U.S. city?

Even when we create a larger number of African-centered schools and home schools throughout the country, who will form the important cadre of teachers and administrators? How do we make sure these individuals remain true to the pedagogy of African-centered curriculum, discipline, and education? How do we prevent the ever-present tendencies of bourgeois values (materialism, individualism, profits over people, pro-imperialist thinking) or patriarchy and homophobia from creeping into and sabotaging our schools, staff, and students? The not-so-subtle answer is that we must create national or regional institutions that recruit and properly train Black people to teach and run African-centered schools, and institutions that accredit such schools.

Simply being a Black teacher does not designate a person as one who works in the interests of Black people, and simply having all Black faculty, staff and students does not characterize a school as being "African-centered." Educators in these schools will need to understand the "Developmental psychology of Black students" (Amos Wilson), African-centered education, and be able to develop disciplinary, management, and instructional methods consistent with this pedagogy. We must provide parents with the capacity to determine if any school is certifiably African-centered beyond just a name or claim.

In closing, Black Nationalists typically argue that "We can't send our children to receive education from our enemies in public schools." Yet, I should remind you that Marcus Garvey, Elijah Muhammad, Ella Baker, Malcolm X, Fred Hampton, Kwame Ture, Assata Shakur, George Jackson, or most of our most radical and committed Black Liberation leaders **did not** attend African-centered schools. They either attended segregated Black schools or integrated schools. In either case, neither brand of these schools was African-centered by our contemporary definition. The creation of African-centered schools was a direct product of the Black Power Movement. Most of these schools did not appear until after the 1970s and later.

This indicates that while African-centered schools are the preferred ideological ideal, such schools are not the only means for producing culturally grounded and empowered Black children. Secondly, our children need an empowering education NOW and we cannot afford to wait several decades to accommodate all of them in such schools. However, we can still help our children emerge competent, committed, and conscious even in the framework of the existing school system if we seriously reconfigure and maximize educational capacity within the larger community village that raises them.

The 7 Objectives of a Revolutionary

The term "Revolutionary" is tossed about so much these days that it has become cliché. Based on my studies and activities throughout the years, revolutionaries have seven important and interrelated missions in an oppressive society.

1. To expose and critique the political, economic, religious and other systems oppressing the masses and educate the masses to how these systems negatively impact their lives, so as to create righteous indignation against oppressive systems and to stimulate a desire among the people to reform or replace them.

2. To expose establishment propaganda, explain it to the people, and help them develop the ability to recognize, understand and counter it.

3. To develop meaningful relationships with the people based on fairness, competence, hard work and accurate information, to create feelings of mutual respect and credibility that will be used to help us love and trust each other and work together in solidarity.

4. To transform the collective consciousness/culture/values of the people to eliminate their own self-defeating, shallow and divisive views and practices and replace them with those that are self-affirming, significant and liberating.

5. To work with the people to dismantle/eliminate oppressive systems and to create alternative systems/institutions to sustain/develop/protect our lives which are based on freedom, justice, and equality (Such systems should not replicate the oppression or injustice in already-existing systems).

6. To develop competent and trustworthy allies in this struggle to enhance our ability to do the tremendous work necessary and destabilize and debilitate oppressive systems at every opportunity.

7. To inspire and develop faith, hope and pride among the people in an effort to counter the negative and spirit-crushing propaganda of the opposition, and to create the capacity of the people to believe in themselves, love themselves and work for themselves.

Agyei Tyehimba, My Two Cents

How to Organize in our Community

On August 9, 2015, The Black Power Cypher (5 Black male educators, organizers and activists from around the United States) did their monthly internet show on the topic, *The Importance of Community Organizing.*[41] We offered some of our own organizing experiences and tips, and we explored how to organize in the Black community

There is perhaps, no topic more timely and relevant in 2015 than organizing the Black community. The great Pan African Marcus Garvey told us, *"Disorganization is the chief enemy of Negro people."* The great Kwame Ture - mentored by Dr. King and Ella Baker - constantly urged us to *"Organize, organize, organize."*

Why Should We Organize in our Community?

---

[41] https://www.youtube.com/watch?v=yjmazPhNB8A

Certainly many of our most effective leaders spend much of their time organizing and encouraging us to do the same. This prompts certain intelligent questions: *"What is the importance of community organizing? How do we benefit from organizing our community?"*

Black people find ourselves beset with a literal flood of problems: failing schools/miseducation, inadequate healthcare, mass incarceration, massive unemployment/poverty and unbridled police brutality. If we submit to cowardice and choose to accept these circumstances, there is nothing more to discuss. However, if we choose to resolve our collective problems and confront those responsible for them, we must advocate for ourselves.

A person can advocate for him/herself individually. A tenant of a residential building for example, can call the management office and complain of receiving inadequate heat during the winter. The management office may not take this one person seriously. Alternatively, the office might solve that one person's heat problem.

Imagine however, if this same tenant contacts other tenants in the building, organizes a tenant association, and 500 people begin complaining to management. They sign petitions, stage protests, solicit legal advice, initiate a rent strike, and attract local media. That management office would be more likely to make sure all tenants receive proper heat.

In other words, organizing multiplies the power of one person *exponentially*.

We can apply this principle to our own history as Black people in the United States. Did Harriet Tubman free 3000 slaves by herself? No. If there were no underground railroad system in place, her efforts would not be as successful. Did Marcus Garvey work alone? No. He had writers, organizers, attorneys, and officers of his organization working together to achieve common goals. Did Martin Luther King singlehandedly coordinate the Civil Rights Movement? No. He worked with fellow ministers, church congregants, college activists, and community organizers all over the country.

The point by now is clear. Organizing our community allows us to *effectively* and *efficiently* solve our collective problems. We can summarize the benefits of organizing as follows:

We enjoy the combined talents, knowledge, resources and experiences of several people.

Our numbers and combined strength persuades others to take our concerns more seriously than they would if we acted alone.

Organizing makes our efforts more powerful and tends to have greater impact (imagine one person boycotting a national department store versus an organization of 200,000 people).

Organizing prevents one person from becoming isolated, fatigued, or attacked. Tasks and responsibilities are shared with several people and committees.

Organizing inspires and empowers entire communities of people and equips entire communities to advocate for themselves. Several people gain new skills, develop courage, and create change; therefore, a movement does not necessarily conclude when one person dies or years pass.

Organizations provide a system of accountability for people. An individual is only accountable to him or herself. However, a person working within an organization is accountable to other members of that organization and the larger community of people they claim to represent or advocate for.

How Do You Organize?

We have briefly addressed the importance of community organizing and the benefits gained from participating in it. But we are now left with the question, *"HOW do we organize in our community?"* In the course of my own teaching, consulting and writing about organizing, people asked me this question literally hundreds of times. Several qualified authors and public speakers address this question. Search the internet and you will come across hundreds or thousands of books, workshops, and speeches on this topic.

This one article cannot and will not provide you with an exhaustive or complete understanding of how to organize. We also need to remember that each issue, campaign or movement is different and may demand different approaches. Nevertheless, we can highlight some central ideas that provide a basic outline for effective community organizing. You can apply this template to your tenant association, parent association, church, nonprofit organization and much more. Additionally, you can research further information to supplement what we provide here.

Identify what it is you care about. Do you want to eliminate gun violence in your neighborhood, address unfair treatment in a local store, provide better educational opportunities for your children, have better heating in your building, rename a city street, or provide food and clothing for homeless people? This is always the first step to organizing in the community, and the basis for all of your subsequent actions, policies, tactics, and strategy.

Determine who else cares about that issue. After identifying your key issue, you must now determine who else in your church, school, building, etc. shares your concern about that issue. If you fail to do this, you will be doing all the work by yourself, and we already addressed the importance of organizing with others. There are several ways you can accomplish this, depending on your energy level and mobility and resources. You can call or e-mail friends, co-workers, classmates, or neighbors. You can knock on doors in your neighborhood. You can create a brief survey and have people complete them. A traditional way to do this is to host a town hall meeting in your community at a place of worship or community center. Make fliers addressing the issue ("Are you concerned about police brutality? Do you want to do something about it?") and distribute those fliers or post them all over your neighborhood. The people who attend this event most likely care about the issue and are willing to address it. In the age of social media, you can post something about the issue on Facebook and see how people respond. Feel free to use whatever method or combination of methods that works best for you. Once you have a group of people who share your concern about an issue, you need to schedule a regular meeting time to discuss and plan.

Create a Mission Statement: It helps to have your group put your reason for organizing and your goal on paper. It is important to have something tangible everyone can refer to in times of disagreement or when clarity and direction are needed.

Have your group identify a goal they want to reach. Sounds easy enough, right? Nevertheless, proceed with caution. Your goal should have certain characteristics if you want to be successful and efficient (avoid wasting precious time and resources). A common method of doing this is to use the **S.M.A.R.T. approach** to goal setting. **SMART** is an easy-to-remember acronym that stands for *Specific, Measurable, Attainable, Relevant,* and *Time-bound.*

Specific: What do we want to accomplish? Who is responsible for resolving the issue? What are the requirements and limitations? **Measurable:** How much, how many, how will we know if we accomplished our goal? **Attainable:** How can we accomplish this goal? Is this a realistic goal based on the tools, skills, constraints and people we have?

Relevant: Is this goal worthwhile and important? Will members of my community be willing to fight to achieve this goal?

Time-Bound: By when do we want to accomplish this goal? What should we do immediately? What should we do long-term?

Create committees to accomplish important tasks: Your group wants to accomplish its goal without wasting time, money or other resources. To do this, you must identify tasks, assign people to complete them, and establish a specific timeline for completion. For example, you may create media, research, finance, and community outreach committees. Each committee or person must have specific tasks to complete. These people or committees need to meet regularly and update your group on their progress, difficulties, and tasks that still need completion.

Identify and develop a strategy and list of tactics to achieve your goal. Your group, based on its goal, research, and resources, must now identify how you will accomplish your goal. This includes but is not limited to: protests, petition-drives, fundraisers, teach-ins, boycotts, demonstrations, press conferences, acts of civil disobedience, proposing and helping to write legislation, editorial articles in the local newspaper, etc.

As we approach the conclusion of this article, there are some important tips I would like to share from my own organizing experience and study:

To be an effective organizer, you must develop authentic relationships with people. You must be concerned about people, interested in their opinions, and you must earn their trust. Otherwise, people will refuse to work with you no matter how prepared and committed you are.

You should be familiar with the community or people you are trying to organize. Where do they hang out? What places of worship do they attend? What people or leaders do they respect? What issues are important to them?

You should not be condescending, arrogant, or the type of person who wants to do everything yourself. Effective organizers are confident yet humble; they know when to talk, and when to listen; they are also inclusive. They actively solicit the support and input of others and are willing to share responsibilities. Their goal is not to become famous, popular or wealthy, but to serve others and help them solve problems. Excellent organizers help other people to gain new skills, confidence, and develop into leaders themselves.

Take time to identify other groups, organizations and individuals who address your issue. If the goal is to reach your goal, it would help to form coalitions with other people as committed to doing this as you are. However, be discerning. All leaders and groups are not what they seem to be. Some are conflicted, compromised and fraudulent. Choose your allies wisely.

Effective organizing is hard work, but you must maintain balance. Human beings are social creatures who need and want time to socialize, have fun and relax. Work hard and be serious about meeting your goals, but also make time for yourself and your group to celebrate victories and socialize.

Encourage critical thinking. Good organizers realize that all opinions or ideas (including their own) are not valid or constructive. Our goal in organizing is not to inflate our egos, impress people with our intelligence, or humiliate anyone; *Our goal is to reach our goal.* Therefore, make time to ask members of your group for respectfully voiced suggestions and critiques. Encourage your group to debate policies and methods to determine the "best" or most effective ones available.

When organizing, it is always important to reach high and challenge yourself. At the same time, we want to make our goals and expectations manageable. If we spread our group too thin or take on too many responsibilities, we demoralize and disappoint our members, fail to meet our goals, and possibly turn people off to organizing in the future. Organizations feel proud when they have several programs or initiatives. However, it is better to do two things exceptionally well, than to do 20 things poorly.

As stated earlier in this article, the information provided here is not enough to make you an effective community organizer, but it is enough to get you started in the right direction. Much success to you in your community organizing efforts, and feel free to contact me with any questions or comments you have about your own community organizing.

Recommended Reading

The Art of Leadership Vol I and II by Oba T'Shaka

Ella Baker & the Black Freedom Movement by Barbara Ransby

The Making of Black Revolutionaries by James Forman

Ready for Revolution: The Life and Struggles of Stokely Carmichael (Kwame Ture) by Kwame Ture

The Activist's Handbook: Winning Social Change in the 21st Century by Randy Shaw

Rules for Radicals by Saul Alinsky

Organizing for Social Change Midwest Academy Manual for Activists by Kemberly Bobo and Steve Max

The Blueprint: A BSU Handbook by Agyei Tyehimba

Who Should Lead Liberation Movements?

Frederick Douglass said something I deeply agree with: "Let he who is wounded cry out." I take this to mean that members of an oppressed group have the prerogative to define, lead, and strategize movements for their liberation.

Naturally, sincere people of privilege can join such movements and participate meaningfully. White communists did important unionizing work with Blacks in the South and provided much-needed media attention and legal defense to Black victims of white violence in the 30s and 40s; White (and Black) Hollywood entertainers coordinated successful fundraisers and lent their star appeal to the

Civil Rights Movement, and white liberals supported with their feet, voices and wallets.

Anti-racism activist Tim Wise speaks forcefully against white privilege; Mark Anthony Neal has challenged what he sees as oppressive aspects of masculinity; Actor Woody Harrelson commits class suicide whenever he speaks out against corporate greed and exploitation; In 1990, renown legal scholar and key theorist of critical race theory, Derrick Bell took a leave of absence from Harvard University to protest the absence of tenured Black female faculty members on its payroll.

There is evidence then, which highlights how privileged people's participation (individually or collectively) benefits social justice or liberation movements. Such cooperation and activism from members of the privileged class in attacking the sources of their own privilege can be very useful to liberation movements by bringing in much-needed resources and attention. Such individuals prove equally effective in educating, organizing and deconstructing the hegemonic practices and institutions of their fellow privileged peers.

However, there are also dangers involved when members of a privileged class champion the oppressed and join movements for their liberation. Often times, privileged people impose their sensibilities, methods and normative standards upon the very people they claim to fight for, thus mirroring the hegemony and arrogance practiced by the powerful forces they presumably oppose.

Additionally, there are cases wherein the oppressed became dependent on the funding and other resources of their privileged supporters, and this dependency alters the goals and tactics of the movement, giving privileged people far too much influence and leading the oppressed to become back-seat drivers in their own liberation struggle. For example, in his famous **"Message to the Grassroots"** speech, Malcolm X explained how white liberal elements compromised the objectives and content of the 1963 March on Washington.

Lastly, members of the privileged class have the luxury of joining and later abandoning liberation movements out of fear or changing political currents. This was certainly the case with the populist leader Thomas Watson who first advocated equality for poor Black farmers during the late 1800s, then later promoted white supremacist ideals to appeal to Southern white voters in the 1900s. Referring to the Black man, he would later write, *"We have to lynch him occasionally, and flog him, now and then, to keep him from blaspheming the Almighty, by his conduct, on account of his smell and his color."*

All liberation movements can benefit from sincere allies including those from the privileged class. However, as Douglass noted, "Those who are wounded should cry out." Men defining themselves as "feminists" can confront their brethren on patriarchy and male privilege. Whites can do anti-racist work in their churches, schools, and community organizations. Affluent but class-rebellious folk can work to educate and organize their wealthy peers. Ultimately, the oppressed must maintain and protect their right to self-determination. They should define their goals and objectives, leadership, and methods, and they should always be the recognized authorities of their own movements.

Women should primarily lead, define, and orchestrate movements against sexism, people of color should primarily lead, define, and orchestrate movements against racism, and the working class and poor should primarily lead, define, and orchestrate movements against corporate/class exploitation. Again, others can join and even help to lead, but they should not dominate or be depended on for resources.

If in our organizing efforts, we come across members of the privileged class who are uncomfortable following our lead, exhibit an obsessive desire to control or dictate policy, and refuse to confront their own hegemonic ideas/practices, we must question their usefulness and relevance to our liberation movements.

The Anatomy of a Protest Movement

Note: This comes from a chapter of my book, *The Blueprint: A BSU Handbook*, in addition to my blog. While the content addresses the college campus scenario, community organizations will find this information relevant as well.

By "movement," I am referring to a sustained and organized struggle on behalf of a group that demands concessions from an agency/institution. This assumes an adversarial or contentious relationship between two parties like the BSU (Black Student Union) and the university for example. The BSU wants a certain thing or set of things, which the university can provide but refuses to for any number of reasons. Therefore, the BSU launches a movement or campaign to get the concessions it wants.

I am disappointed with those Black Students Unions around the country that have become social clubs rather than the agents of resistance and empowerment they were founded to be on college campuses. I want to inspire a return to that original BSU spirit. This chapter will equip your organization to take its rightful place in the tradition of BSUs by acquainting you with the "anatomy" so to speak, of a protest movement.

We might say that a campaign is composed of eight general parts: *Irreconcilable Discontent, Research, Propaganda, a Call to action, Presentation of demands, Outreach & Alliance Building, Confrontation, and Negotiation.*

Irreconcilable Discontent: This refers to a mentality or psychological state that leads people to create a movement to confront the university or any other power structure. People may experience discontent with a situation for several years but never do anything to resolve their conflicts because they have "made peace" with it in one way or another. They might rationalize that this "is just the way things are," or that "we can't win" or refuse to seriously address the issue out of fear or personal discomfort.

However, irreconcilable discontent takes place when an incident occurs that is so egregious, so blatantly insulting or oppressive that people overcome their fears and skepticism and feel compelled to respond in organized fashion. For example, Black people have resented the ominous presence and brutal activities of police in our communities for decades. We detest police harassing Black motorists, stopping and frisking our youth, and shooting us down in the streets.

We know this is unjust and criminal; we know that the officers responsible go free and resume their presence on the police force.

Yet despite our discontent, we reconcile with such practices, telling ourselves to "let the system do its job," or that "God will punish them." As demonstrated in our response to Trayvon Martin's murder on February 26, 2012, and his murderer's subsequent exoneration, we participate in a few marches or petition drives, hold some press conferences and rallies, and eventually go back to business as usual.

Irreconcilable discontent means "the straw has broken the camel's back," we come to the realization that "Enough is enough," and we are compelled to act in an assertive manner (even to the point of breaking oppressive rules/laws and refusing to cooperate with societal convention).

In Montgomery, Alabama, Black people in the 1950s were accustomed to sitting in the segregated section of the bus. We were accustomed to paying our fare, then exiting to board the bus via the back door. Often the bus drivers pulled off with us standing there. We did not like this mistreatment. We were discontent for sure, but we mumbled under our breath, accepting that this obvious form of injustice was "just the way things were" at that time. Of course, some individuals refused to comply with these laws, but Blacks did not collectively wage a movement.

However, when innocent and well-respected seamstress and longtime activist Rosa Parks was roughly taken off the bus and arrested for not complying with the law, Blacks in Montgomery became **irreconcilably discontented**. This sense of outrage led to a

381-day bus boycott that nearly brought the bus company to bankruptcy and led to a court decision banning bus segregation.

Successful campaigns or movements usually begin when our people feel a sense of outrage so intense that they are ready and willing to take action. Astute leaders anticipate or recognize such moments and begin organizing this widespread anger and frustration into a sustained and organized movement for social or political change.

Research: At some point, organizers and activists begin researching to determine who is responsible for resolving the issue, methods they can take to bring attention to the issue, and what specific demands they will make to the parties that have the power to resolve the issue.

Call to Action: Having defined the issues, and "opposition force" responsible for resolving them, the organizers and activists issue a call to action to the masses, directly calling upon them to move beyond discontent and into organized action. During this early phase of your movement, you will hold meetings with your group to effectively explain how this issue affects your members, why they should be outraged, and give them a sense of their power to resolve the issue.

Presentation of Demands: After concluding your research to clarify the issues involved and party responsible, and issuing your call-to-action, you formally present your grievances and demands to the responsible party. You can do this in several ways, including a petition, letter, or verbally at a meeting with the person you identify as the appropriate party. This is obviously the main goal of your movement, namely to get your demands satisfied. In the best case, the opposition agrees to your demands in writing on its official letterhead. This is not very likely to happen immediately however, as powerful organizations tend to underestimate the seriousness or validity of your cause and do not respond well to changing their policies or practices.

Outreach & Alliance Building: Anticipating a long struggle, your organization contacts other groups and leaders for support and resources to aid in your movement. This lends greater numbers and therefore strength to your cause. You want to identify campus and community organizations to support you. If you have been building relations with these people in advance (as I suggested earlier) this step will prove easier and more successful.

Propaganda: In an effort to heighten and dramatize the tension surrounding the issue, organizers use propaganda. Through informational fliers, press conferences and rallies, they use colorful language and imagery to expose the contradictions involved, highlight the specific injustice(s), and call for the responsible parties to take corrective action. Your propaganda should powerfully describe and detail the injustice, identify your grievances and demands, and explain how and why your demands went unmet.

During this phase, it is important that the organization identify an individual as their opposition or responsible party. A corporation, university or other institution might be responsible, but you must put a face on that institution, as people cannot effectively confront an abstract "company." Your research should have discovered one person (a CEO, university president, or elected official who is representative of the organization you are going to confront). During this phase, you will want to write editorials in your college, organization and community newspapers and give press conferences detailing your issue. You want everyone to clearly understand what you are fighting for and how it affects you and others.

Confrontation: In this phase of the movement or campaign the disgruntled organization directly confronts the individual (representative of the institution) believed to be responsible for creating or at least resolving the issue. Naturally, this only occurs if your grievances and demands are initially unmet. To encourage sympathy from outside observers and to develop proper momentum, you should begin with simple, less intense and more "respectable" tactics (petitions, meetings, rallies, newspaper articles) and if necessary, become increasingly more intense, dramatic and assertive.

If the opposition does not respond to these tactics and you are compelled to engage in more assertive measures, other people not involved in your movement will more likely understand and support your cause. They will also be more likely to view your opposition as being unreasonable and unfair. This perception and sympathy may come in handy later in your campaign when you need all the outside support you can get. When your tactics become more aggressive, the court of public opinion will be more sensitive to your cause. If you conduct your most assertive action too early in the campaign, and the opposition does not flinch, your campaign loses momentum and it may be close to impossible to regain it.

Confrontations typically consist of specific tactics. These may include petitions, letter-writing campaigns, rallies, building takeovers, marches, and mass phone calls of complaint/concern to the individual/institution, demonstrations and protests.

Petitions are concise letters that clearly specify the issues involved, your grievances and demands, and the person/institution you deem responsible for addressing your issue. These letters have space at the bottom for your supporters to sign in agreement with your petition demands.

The strength of a petition lies in the number of people that sign it. It shows that your organization has a large and diverse base of support, and puts pressure on the opposition to take your matter seriously and to resolve it. Because each person that signs your petition reads it first, a petition is also an excellent way to inform the public about your organization and the issue you are fighting for. Petition drives often result in people joining or becoming supportive of your organization. A petition puts the opposition on notice that you are in disagreement with a policy, procedure or situation so that they cannot claim ignorance later. It also creates a documented record of your dispute. A well-orchestrated petition drive will often lead to a meeting with the opposition and in the best case, concessions from the opposition. Online petitions, which you can create free on websites like Change.org, Petitiononline.com, or ipetitions.com, are powerful petition tools, because people can "sign" them with a click of a button and you can arrange it so that every time a person signs, a copy of the petition is emailed to the person you designate.

Letter-writing campaigns constitute another good tactic because they lead people to become involved in your movement and demonstrate your broad base of support. With this tactic, you provide people with a sample of the issues, injustice involved, and your grievance/demands and allow them to create a brief letter supporting your cause. These days, you would most likely use email to accomplish this.

Rallies are (usually) outdoor meetings held in a high-traffic area on campus or in the community. You have various leaders and activists from your group and others speak on your movement and what you are fighting for. Your primary goal is to educate the public and generate support. For added effectiveness, you can have tables at your rally site where people sign your petitions or receive more information about your organization. These types of events tend to attract media coverage, which promotes your movement to people who know little to nothing about it. You will want to invite powerful and informed speakers who are respected by the community and list their names on your fliers promoting the event. Their followers and supporters will come to hear them speak which helps you gain even more supporters. Effective rallies are informative and dynamic. The audience should be encouraged to chant (i.e. "No justice, no peace!" "A people united will never be defeated") sing protest songs hold signs and applaud loudly.

Building Takeovers are forms of protest that are very dramatic, controversial, attention grabbing, and usually illegal. However, because this involves disrupting a place of business and because it is intimidating to workers in the building, this tactic is risky. It can create enemies among innocent workers who may not understand or agree with your issue, brand your organization as violent or coercive, and lead to destruction of property or even minor injuries. Institutions generally ban takeovers so you face the very real likelihood of arrests. This tactic MUST be well organized and you must clearly communicate dos and don'ts for your participants or this can backfire in very negative ways for your movement.

Marches involve a large number of people walking in unison to a designated place where an organization usually holds a rally. Marches are accompanied by colorful signs with headlines that dramatize your issue. You can organize singing and chanting as people march or do a silent march. These are excellent for generating media coverage and attracting the attention of passers-by who wonder what all the commotion is about. Because they involve large audiences, march conveners should make sure the event is well organized. You must inform participants beforehand what route they will use, what the destination is and what the issue is. In addition, you should have a spokesperson on hand to speak with reporters and answer questions.

Mass phone calls are self-explanatory. You provide hundreds of people with the work phone number of your opposition figure (calling their home or cell phone might be seen as a form of harassment) and a few basic scripts to read when the person (or their assistant) answers. Each person calls and explains his/her concern about your issue. Then they ask what this person plan to do about it. This is a legal and completely easy way to disrupt the individual's workday while reinforcing your issue. When done correctly, this tactic ties up your opposition's phone lines and makes it difficult for them to conduct business as usual. Even if no one answers, your callers can leave a message. This pressure tactic demonstrates your strength and wide base of support. It also subtly pressures them to resolve your issue. I like to call this tactic 'Holding the phone lines hostage."

Demonstrations represent another dramatic tactic that draw media coverage for your issue and involve great fun. You can think of a demonstration as social theater. People using this tactic dramatize the said issue in very creative and engaging ways designed to describe (in exaggerated fashion) exactly why and how the institution, policy or practice is oppressive, exploitive or simply unfair. Students protesting a tuition hike might stage a demonstration in which a college class has a professor lecturing to only three students who happen to be wealthy and pampered. This is designed to illustrate the organization's belief that the proposed tuition increase will significantly reduce the student population and make the college affordable only to affluent students. A BSU protesting a policy that ends affirmative action on their campus might stage a funeral scene. Pallbearers solemnly carry a casket marked "Black Students at this university." Once inside the mock funeral home, the preacher begins to deliver a moving eulogy for Black students on campus, noting that the removal of affirmative action "killed" the presence of Blacks on campus. Nearby, in a mock court scene, we see a prosecutor grilling the university president and accusing him of "murdering" affirmative action. A Black-student jury pronounces him guilty and the university president is led out of court in handcuffs. As you might imagine, these demonstrations dramatize the perceived injustices involved in ways that are more fun and sensational than would be the case in a rally or petition. They also guarantee media coverage and depict the opposition in a negative light. By definition, demonstrations involve the skillful use of propaganda.

Negotiation: Usually the last phase of a successful campaign involves a series of meetings between a BSU representative (usually the president and a Vice President) and a representative of the opposition. At this point, the institution has suffered great embarrassment in the media and tremendous pressure from the BSU and its supporters. In an effort to continue operating normally and end its public embarrassment and increasingly aggressive BSU protests and demonstrations, the opposing institution is now compelled to sit with your organization to bring the movement to an end by making concessions.

In most cases, the negotiating phase involves some degree of compromise and flexibility from the protesting organization. Sometimes budgetary considerations or other realities make some demands untenable or impractical. In these cases, the BSU will have to determine which demands are most important and non-negotiable. After these meetings, all agreements made verbally must be put in writing and signed by a person with the authority to grant the requests and the BSU official. It is important to establish reasonable dates by which these changes will be implemented, or the university has wiggle room to renege on their agreements.

In conclusion, please realize that no movement or campaign unfolds in one specific manner. This anatomy of a campaign I provided cannot possibly account for or anticipate every single nuance of a struggle. It does however acquaint you with the general things you should consider and for which you should prepare.

Rethinking the Goals and Methods of Child Education

Wouldn't it be interesting if we approached child education in the same manner as preparing a fictional Jedi Knight? This would require us to shift our focus from merely protecting, feeding, clothing, and teaching basic lessons, to preparing our children with the specific SKILLS, CHARACTER TRAITS, and ATTITUDES they would need to function effectively as adults and to defend and advance our communities long after we're gone.

Notwithstanding white supremacy, the reason why so many of our young people find themselves lost, confused, and dysfunctional in the world is that we as their parents are not properly preparing them, nor are the institutions in the proverbial community "village."

Frankly speaking, the vast majority of our children are ill equipped, and this sad reality manifests through the consistently poor decisions they make, their immaturity, their lack of initiative and motivation, and their inability to generally deal with life successfully. Moreover, this reality will continue until we become proactive in our parenting and creative in our approach to education. Essentially, such thinking would completely transform education as we know it, and result in the training of balanced and well-rounded young people, leaders and problem-solvers.

Is there a precedent for this? In most ancient cultures, children had to undergo rites of initiation in which they were not considered an adult until they received certain training, passed several tests and demonstrated proficiency in the skills and qualities their village needed for survival and development. For instance, an initiate would learn how to hunt, build shelter, skin an animal for clothing, fight, and a number of other things. Wouldn't it be interesting if our homes, schools and spiritual centers approached education in this way? We would identify the skills and qualities our children and need in the "real" world, create lessons and projects to impart such knowledge and skills, then test them to determine if they are adequately prepared. Some of these tests would be traditional written tests. Most trials would involve actually having to do something, avoid something, go without something, create something, withstand something, and so on. In short, this transformed educational process would be both abstract and functional. Wouldn't preparation like this help to ensure that they grow into powerful and competent adults? Wouldn't students and children be more willing to learn with such engaging and relevant activities?

In the epic Movie series "Star Wars," the ancient rites of passage custom is captured through the training of "Jedi Knights," warrior monks sworn to protect the galaxy and promote peace and cooperation. Initiates undergo a series of lessons and training, which conclude with a series of trials they must overcome. These trials cover five areas including the Trial of Skill, the Trial of Courage, the Trial of the Flesh, the Trial of Spirit, and the Trial of Insight or Knowledge.

Living as we do in contemporary times with a specific cultural, political and economic context, our training program would need some tweaking to be relevant. Perhaps such skills and qualities would include:

- Cleaning and organizing the home

- Cooking well-balanced, delicious and nutritious meals

- Creating a business

- Self-Defense (including martial arts and use of weapons)

- Nonviolent conflict mediation

- Reading and writing effectively

- Public Speaking

- Prioritizing issues

- Budgeting money

- Managing time

- Controlling emotions

- Logic and Debate

- Chess

- Physical fitness

- Concentration

- Patience

- Meditation

- Social Studies (Political Science, Geography, Economics, Civics, History, Anthropology)

- Science

- Mathematics

- Creating a plan to achieve goals

- Fasting (from food and speaking)

- Critical Thinking

- Farming

- Hygiene and grooming

- Spiritual development

- Community service

Call it impractical if you wish, but I am convinced that our educational system as it currently exists is outdated, largely irrelevant and clearly failing. If we want our children to be prepared for the future, then quite simply, we must determine the skills, information and qualities they need to function effectively as adults, and create a structure and culture that prepares them accordingly. Not only will a system like this produce genuine leaders and problem-solvers, but also the students would likely find this approach fun, engaging and relevant.

Revolutionary Black Love

Like countless numbers of Black people before me, I affirm our constitutional and human rights as Black people to defend ourselves in the face of unrelenting brutality and murder by racist police, white vigilantes and predatory members of our own communities. Our capacity to "police" our own communities increases when we cultivate *revolutionary love* for each other.

I agreed completely. I often quote the iconic Argentine revolutionary Che Guervara who once wrote: *"At the risk of seeming ridiculous, let me say that the true revolutionary is guided by a great feeling of love. It is impossible to think of a genuine revolutionary lacking this quality."*

Our powerfully insightful intellectual James Baldwin noted, *"The sea rises, the light fails, lovers cling to each other, and children cling to us. The moment we cease to hold each other, the moment we break faith with one another, the sea engulfs us and the light goes out."*

Moved by this response to my Facebook post, and by the above quotes, I began thinking deeply about the phrase. I asked myself, "What does revolutionary Black love look like, how do we cultivate it, and how will its existence impact how we relate to each other as Black people?"

What Does Revolutionary Black Love Look Like?

I begin with the following premise: *"Revolutionary Black love is a redundant phrase. For In a society that has spent and continues to spent countless effort and energy teaching Black people to hate themselves, the very existence of Black love itself is by definition, revolutionary."* Yet this point still does not help us understand or describe Revolutionary Black love. To accomplish this, I dive into my own life for answers, and the larger ocean of Black experience itself.

- My mother demonstrated revolutionary Black love when she sacrificed stylish clothes, a graduate scholarship to New York University, a larger apartment, and having additional children, in order to finance a private education for me from elementary school to high school (and compelled my dad to agree with her decision). This twelve-year commitment demonstrated that she prioritized her child's education over personal comfort and other interests.

- My dad was a native New Yorker and Harlemite who played for basketball powerhouse Benjamin Franklin High School alongside the legendary Earl "The Goat" Manigault (He also regularly played in the famed Rucker's Basketball Tournament with the likes of Nate Archibald, Lew Alcindor a.k.a. Kareem Abdul-Jabbar, Charlie Scott, "Pee Wee" Kirkland, and a number of other Harlem basketball icons). He told me that his high school coach – who was also the assistant principal – let him and other ball players skip class. The coach would unethically assign them undeserved good grades to keep them eligible to play basketball. Consequently, my dad's academic skills suffered and he struggled with reading. Nonetheless, he later got help and became a prolific reader (his collection of books on African civilizations, Benin art, slavery, and Malcolm X became my first library on the Black experience). When I decided to apply to Syracuse University for undergraduate study, my dad learned about the H.E.O.P. program, contacted the assistant director, and arranged an interview with her. He told me to write an essay explaining why I wanted to attend (despite my protests that I had already done son as part of the application process). He rented a car and drove me 4 hours to Syracuse, New York where we met with Mrs. Betty Boozer. She, no doubt awed by my charismatic and determined dad, and by my essay and eagerness, pulled strings and got me into the program. Later I became a radical and controversial student leader at the university, helping to lead several months of protests, building takeovers, and meeting disruptions. A university official called my house on behalf of the university, explaining that my political activities were causing great embarrassment to the school and might end with me being expelled. My dad later recalled the incident to me. "This administrator from Syracuse University called, saying you were a trouble-maker and you were embarrassing the school with all those demonstrations, taking over buildings, and rallies. He said to tell you to resign from president of your organization or they might kick you out. I told him, that your mother and I were proud of you, and that you have our **full** support. If the university does not like your protests, they should make sure you have nothing to protest about. I told him the next time he calls me, it better be to apologize, and I hung up." My dad demonstrated revolutionary love by doing all he could to get me in college, and then supporting our Black student movement and my role in it, even with threats of me being kicked out. Through action, he taught me to stand up for our people and stick your neck out, even at expense to yourself.

I can continue with countless examples from my personal life, but revolutionary Black love is well documented in our collective experience as Africans in America. Harriet Tubman who made dozens of trips to and from the South, rescued 3000 Black people from the horrors of chattel slavery. She did this at great risk to herself and a $50,000 bounty on her head; Ella Baker was a tireless and brilliant organizer dating back to work with the Young Negroes Cooperative League in the 1930s. She later worked with the NAACP, SCLC, SNCC and a host of other organizations for almost five decades, up to her death in 1986. Hear her for yourself in the clip below.

Baker organized a conference at Shaw University in 1960 to coordinate the efforts of student activists around the country. SCLC hoped this would lead to a student wing of their organization. Baker instead encouraged the assembled student activists to form their own independent organization and use their own voice and ideas. The Student Nonviolent Coordinating Committee (SNCC) was born and went on to radicalize the Civil Rights Movement, and make it more inclusive of Black women. Rather than emphasizing charismatic male leadership, SNCC focusing on grassroots organizing and inclusive leadership. They went all over the south teaching leadership and organizing skills to poor Black folks, many of whom were previously inactive until SNCC's contact. We might not know the names or benefit from the activism of Julian Bond, Stokely Carmichael (Kwame Ture), Dianne Nash, Bernice Johnson Reagon, Marion Barry, Bob Moses, James Foreman, or H. Rap Brown were it not for SNCC and Baker's political mentorship. Baker demonstrated Revolutionary Black love by spending her life in service to Black people and by mentoring youth and allowing them to make their own decisions and determine their own leadership. Bernice Johnson Reagon was so moved by Baker's mentorship and tireless service that she wrote a song in her tribute entitled "Ella's Song," which she performs with her group "Sweet Honey in the Rock."

We can summarize that revolutionary Black love involves:

- Fearlessness: Not allowing fears of persecution to stop us from taking principled stands.
- Agency: A willingness to roll up one's sleeves and get personally involved in listening to others and working with others to address day-to-day issues and larger community concerns.
- Selflessness: Putting community needs over personal comfort.
- Empowering and supporting those in our immediate and community family and making this a priority.

- Being patient and nurturing with our young people, providing them with mentorship and skills building, and then trusting them to develop their own leadership and ideas.
- Acting immediately to address current issues, but planning to bring future visions into fruition.

How do we cultivate it?

The answer to this question is simple, but practicing it takes patience and consistent work. To cultivate Revolutionary Black love, we must begin by valuing and loving ourselves. This includes loving our bodies/physical features, our history and heritage, and our freedom and empowerment. We must through knowledge and education, break through artificial layers of self-hate and devaluation created for us by those who mistreat and exploit us. We must also be honest with ourselves about our shortcomings, contradictions, and self-defeating behavior. Then we work hard to be and do better. In the process, we gain humility, as we recognize that we are fragile, prone to mistakes and errors in judgment like anyone else. This leads us to apologize when we violate another member of the community, without feeling inferior or weak for doing so.

The next stage involves extending that personal love, honesty and humility to our people. We begin to want for our community what we want for ourselves and our families. We put ourselves in position to render excellent service to our larger communities, and we do so not with a sense of entitlement or arrogance, but with a sense of humility. As we begin to help others without strings attached, we develop trust. As we provide constructive criticism without condescension or judgment, we become community mentors whose advice people trust and actively seek. We empathize with the challenges, pain, and frustrations of our community members. We develop a capacity to solve personal and collective problems and work together despite differences of opinion. We listen when others speak and do not take offense because we know they have only positive and loving intentions. We also learn to disagree without attacking or insulting one another in doing so. We develop the empowering capacity to forgive our brothers and sisters, and to resolve conflicts without resorting to violence. In other words, we become "Our brother's and sister's keeper."

How will Revolutionary Black love impact our community?

As we begin to value ourselves and our people, as we begin to show empathy, compassion, and concern, as we become fearless, community service-oriented, and selfless, we can expect to notice the following:

- Black people willingly share their knowledge, money, and other resources to help each other in noble and authentic efforts.

- We protect and stand up for each other even if we ourselves have not been mistreated.

- We unashamedly identify and expose those in or outside of our community who work against our common interests, or who are fraudulent.

- We support noble Black organizations, movements, and leaders who work to improve conditions for us, even if we do not fully agree with their methods or ideas. In such cases, we choose organizations/movement that closely align with our beliefs, and support them while challenging them to be better and do better.

- We take positions or create projects to empower our people, even when doing so causes controversy, or persecution to ourselves.

- We empower, mentor our youth, and give them opportunities to lead and solve problems.

- We state our disagreements with policy, methods, and people clearly and respectfully because doing so makes our movements, organizations, and communities better.

I thank sister Loga Michelle Odom for sharing the phrase "Revolutionary Black love," and I encourage us to really think about the information/ideas put forth in this article. Hate, envy, apathy, distrust, and cynicism are choices we make. So too is Revolutionary Black Love. This love, and the various expressions of it, is indispensable and unavoidable if we truly desire to be fulfilled, successful, and FREE. The doors of Revolutionary Black love are open.....who will come?

Tribute to Chokwe Lumumba

When word came that Chokwe Lumumba -the recently elected Mayor of Jackson, Mississippi – died of heart failure on February 25, 2014, most Black people had not even heard of him.

Those who were familiar with Lumumba, knew him as a proud Black man ("New Afrikan"), revolutionary, attorney for Black political prisoners (including Assata Shakur and Geronimo Pratt), founder of the Malcolm X Grassroots Movement, and former Vice President of the Republic of New Afrika. Given his tremendous contributions to Black people, this article will highlight Lumumba as the consummate organizer and revolutionary he was. Given the widespread media blackout of Lumumba, his Mayoral win, and his general significance yo us, this is most important. There are at least four things we should all know about brother Chokwe Lumumba in order to understand his monumental significance:

1. **He was a revolutionary and important figure of the Black Power Movement.** Chokwe served in official capacity as a member of the **Republic of New Afrika,** which was a Black Nationalist organization that among other things, A.) Called for America to pay Black people reparations for centuries of Black unpaid labor and suffering and B.) Demanded an acknowledged an independent Black nation created from the states of South Carolina, Georgia, Alabama, Mississippi, and Louisiana. Lumumba served as Minister of Justice and Vice President of the organization. Founded and headed by Milton Henry (later Gaidi Abiodun Obadale) the RNA was an important organization created during the Black Power Movement.

2. **He was a humanitarian and activist attorney.** In 1975, Lumumba graduated Cum Laude from Wayne State University Law School in Detroit, Michigan. Three years later, he began his own law firm. For the next few decades, he would go on to represent Assata Shakur, Geronimo Pratt, Fulani Sunni Ali, and several other wrongly accused Black activists.

3. **He was an institution-builder.** As an undergraduate at Kalamazoo College, he formed the Black United Front to push for the formation of Black Studies Departments in the late 60s. In 1987, he co-founded **N'COBRA** (National Coalition of Blacks for

Reparations in America). He also went on to help create the Malcolm X Grassroots Movement.

4. He was a public servant. From 2009-2013, Lumumba served on the Jackson, Mississippi City Council and on June 4, 2013 was elected Mayor of Jackson, Mississippi, which had a former reputation for virulent racism. I suggest you watch the episode of Democracy Now that covered Lumumba's life.[42]

With all of this activist history and public service background, why was Chokwe Lumumba so anonymous to Black people in America? How come so few Black folk I spoke to even recognized his name? *Precisely because of his organizing and activist history!* To give Lumumba media coverage would be to raise awareness of an educated and conscious revolutionary who boldly advocated for Black people, never sold out, compromised his politics, or abandoned his mission over several decades.

These are qualities sorely lacking in leadership today, particularly in Black elected officials. I suspect the corporate media was none-to-eager to reinvigorate a national discussion on reparations, Black Nationalism, and independent Black politics. Therefore, they simply did not cover it. Strangely enough, they were much more vigilant about reporting his sudden and unexpected death.....

---

[42]

http://www.democracynow.org/2014/2/26/chokwe_lumumba_remembering_americ as_most_revolutionary

Brother Lumumba's election excited many of us who saw his victory as an important historical precedent: An uncompromised Black Nationalist and humanitarian with a proven level of community commitment and loyalty, elected as Mayor of a southern city! We anxiously followed him, looking forward to both his policies and their reception. People like myself who see some potential in local politics, believe Lumumba's win signalled a tactic we should explore in other municipalities with majority Black populations. I saw in him a tangible expression and manifestation of the independent political spirit, protest, and institution-building brother Malcolm spoke about. Sadly, brother Lumumba's mission was prematurely aborted when he died on February 25. 2014.

Yet the struggle continues. Salute to this great man, whose life ended before his mission! May the Creator and ancestors be pleased with him and bless his family, and may **we learn from and continue his legacy**.....

Conclusion

I took great care to choose articles from my blog that were relevant to the Black community, informative and inspiring. I truly hope you found these writings to be such.

These writings constitute a broad summary of my sociopolitical thought. At minimum, these essays can form the basis of focused study groups in our community. I'd also like to see these ideas debated within our organizations. It does not matter whether one agrees or disagrees with any of my perspectives. What matters is that we build the capacity to think critically, discard what we cannot use, and implement what we can. As the National Director of Education for "Souljahs of the People," I plan to use parts of this book in our own political education curriculum.

I am no armchair or Ivy Tower intellectual who writes and thinks simply for sport. Everything I write addresses issues I find important and useful for the liberation of our people. Brother Malcolm's call for us to "Wake up, Clean up, and Stand up," rings in my ears every day. In addition, it is this call that I attempt to address in my own writings, organizing efforts, and public speeches.

I am interested in your thoughts concerning these writings, and I encourage you to share your thoughts with me at truself143@gmail.com. I also encourage you to visit Amazon.com and write a review for *My Two Cents* so that others may benefit from your perspective and experience. Thank you for your support, and keep pushing for Black Consciousness, Black Solidarity and Black Power!

About the Author

 Agyei Tyehimba is an educator, author and activist born and raised in Harlem, New York. Agyei is co-founder of a middle school in the Bronx, NY named KAPPA Middle School 215. Agyei was a student leader at Syracuse and Cornell Universities. For the past 30 years, Agyei has educated Black and Latino youth, taught parents how to advocate for their children, taught community residents and college students how to organize and challenge white supremacy, and delivered speeches and workshops across the country.

He has written three books ("Game Over: The Rise and Transformation of a Harlem Hustler," "The Blueprint: A BSU Handbook," and "Truth for our Youth: A Self Empowerment Book for Teens." He has been featured on C-Span, NY1 News, HuffPost Live, and a documentary entitled "Alpo Martinez: The Mayor of Harlem on the A&E Network.

Currently Agyei writes a popular blog entitled "My True Sense," and is the Founder and Director of Harlem Liberation School. Agyei is a co-founder of "Souljahs of the People," and serves as its National Director of Education.

Agyei earned his Bachelor's Degree in sociology from Syracuse University, his Master's Degree in Africana Studies from Cornell University, and his Master's Degree in Afro-American Studies from the University of Massachusetts at Amherst.

Learn more about Agyei Tyehimba by visiting his website:

http://truself143.wix.com/agyeityehimba

Subscribe to his YouTube Channel:

https://www.youtube.com/user/truself143

Follow on Twitter: @agyei143

Learn about his new organization "Souljahs of the People"

http://truself143.wix.com/souljahz

Visit Harlem Liberation School

https://www.smore.com/r5t4b

www.ingramcontent.com/pod-product-compliance
Lightning Source LLC
Chambersburg PA
CBHW070853290526
45795CB00001B/100